LEADERSHIP CHARISMA

Leadership Charisma

Bud Haney & Jim Sirbasku
with Deiric McCann

S&H
PUBLISHING
COMPANY LLC.

S & H Publishing Company
5205 Lake Shore Drive
Waco, Texas 76710-1732
USA
Tel: + 1 (254) 751 1644
Fax: +1 (254) 772 8155

First Edition

ISBN   978-0-9742221-8-9 (Hard Cover)
ISBN   978-0-9742221-9-6 (Soft Cover)

Printed in the United States by Signature Book Printing, Gaithersburg, MD 20879

ORDERING

Quantity Sales
Discounts are available to corporations or others purchasing in large quantities. For details, please contact S & H Publishing Company at the address above.

Individual Sales
S & H publications are available through all good bookstores, from Amazon.com, and directly from S & H Publishing Company (contact details above).

College textbook/course use; orders by US trade bookstores and wholesalers
Please contact S & H Publishing Company (contact details above).

Editing: Alicia McAuley Publishing Services (www.aliciamcauley.com)
Proofreading: The Grammar Geek (www.thegrammargeek.com)
Design and Layout: Alicia McAuley Publishing Services (www.aliciamcauley.com)
Original Photographs: Deasy Photographic (www.deasyphotographystudio.ie)
Jacket Design: Steve Kadjan (web.me.com/stevekadjan)
Model (Chapter 8): Karen Houlihan

Endorsements for
Leadership Charisma

"*L*EADERSHIP *CHARISMA* LOOKS at a style of leadership long presumed to be unattainable for most people not 'naturally' born 'charismatic' … and gives people real, tangible, and quantifiable tools and behaviors they can immediately use to increase their personal effectiveness. This is one of the few resources I know that delves deeply into why this style of leadership is so effective, how it can be used and applied by anyone, and how it can be implemented in any organization. If you are looking for a resource that will help you passionately share a vision and purpose – and enlist others to help you make that happen – this book is for you."

— Brad Sugars, founder and chairman, ActionCOACH

"Through research, insights and stories, Bud and Jim have taken the mystery out of what it takes to become an effective and charismatic leader. They have created a blueprint that is brilliantly organized and insanely easy to follow. Just add your own commitment and hard work and you are on your way to leadership success."

— Sam Reese, CEO, Miller Heiman

"*Leadership Charisma* addresses one of the most important and often overlooked parts of leadership: building a style of behavior and communication that inspires, motivates, and brings people together toward the organization's goals."

— Josh Bersin, president and CEO, Bersin & Associates

"Yes! Charismatic leaders can be created and this book explains how to do it. A must-read for anyone who manages others. Enlightening, effective, and easy to follow."

— Mark Hamdan, CEO, HRsmart

"From the title of the book, *Leadership Charisma*, one thinks, 'What on earth could they write about? Either leaders have charisma or they don't.' After the first chapter, you quickly realize that leadership charisma can be learned. The authors have done an excellent job of succinctly yet thoroughly explaining how to develop charisma and how to discern when others have it. A quick and effective read."

— Pamela Hernandez, executive vice president, operations and strategy, Woodmen of the World

"This is a book that has all the answers to your questions. If you want to get ahead, it is a must-read!"

— Bernard Rapoport, chairman emeritus and founder, American Income Life Insurance Company

"I strongly believe that organizational culture and values drive success and the organizational leader sets the tone. Research to define the behaviors that can generate such leadership charisma, and, therefore, help leaders set the tone, is key to redefining organizations. Kudos to Bud Haney and Profiles International for developing this research!"

— Dana Gibson, PhD, CPA, president, Sam Houston State University

"Leaders can be made and *Leadership Charisma* offers a roadmap. Years of research and experience at Profiles International have yielded an invaluable guide for people wishing to develop or improve their leadership skills. It is applicable professionally in the largest of businesses as well as personally in the home for those wishing to improve parenting skills. *Leadership Charisma* should be required reading for anyone who leads or wants to lead a group, large or small."

— David Sibley, DDS, MSD, JD, former state senator, Texas

"*Leadership Charisma* is the ultimate read for those seeking to reach the summit in personal leadership development."

— Joe Fertitta, senior vice president, western regional marketing,
MGM Marketing

"Ever since I was a young boy, Bud Haney and Jim Sirbasku have embodied the very essence of success and leadership. Their unique blend of passion and motivation influenced my life for the better, and I know others will benefit greatly following their examples."

— Jim Dunnam, District 57, state representative, State of Texas

Dedication

W<small>E WERE JUST</small> three months into writing this book when Jim Sirbasku, my business partner and best friend of 40 years, passed away suddenly.

Jim had an enormous impact on the lives of everyone he came to know. In announcing Jim Sirbasku Day, Terry Stephens, chairman of the Waco Chamber of Commerce, opened his talk with words that summed Jim up perfectly:

> The thing I remember most about Jim Sirbasku was his enthusiasm. When you met Jim Sirbasku, whether it was the first time or the hundredth time, he was glad to see you – and you knew he was glad to see you.
>
> His persona was one of enthusiasm and high energy, and he poured that energy into the people he met and the people he worked with ...

There is no act more charismatic than making people enthusiastic and hungry for life.

Jim's energy and enthusiasm were some of the classic charismatic qualities this book talks about, and his larger-than-life and hugely charismatic spirit lives on in each and every one of these pages.

This book is dedicated to Jim's memory on behalf of the tens of thousands of people whose lives he touched – and who will always feel his loss deeply.

Bud Haney
January 3, 2011

Contents

The Importance of Leadership Charisma

W OULD YOU LIKE to dramatically improve the results you get from the people who work for you, become dramatically more productive and successful, and at the same time develop an impact on others that sets you apart from all other leaders around you?

Would you like to be one of those leaders who seem to have a natural gift with everyone they meet, which makes them more successful in all aspects of their business and personal lives? That's what leadership charisma can do for you.

The world of business has seen some tough times over the last few years, and in these challenging times all of us have struggled to come up with a magic formula for success. There is just one formula for achievement in modern business – get your people onboard and invested in your success and the success of your organization. All other things being equal, business success comes down to people.

If your employees are totally dedicated to the business, if they buy into the organization's vision and are prepared to do all that they can to ensure that this vision comes to pass, then the business is more likely to be successful.

This is why the concept of "employee engagement" has garnered so much attention over the last few years. As you'll see shortly, leadership charisma and employee engagement are inextricably linked. In fact, it is extraordinary that this is the first book ever to identify that link and to detail how forward-looking leaders can exploit it to extract tremendous productivity from willing people.

The Conference Board defines employee engagement perfectly as: "a heightened emotional connection that an employee feels for his or her organization, that influences him or her to exert greater discretionary effort to his or her work."

The Towers Perrin Global Workforce Study surveyed nearly 90,000 employees in 18 countries. They observed:

In one recent study we looked at fifty global companies over a year, correlating their employee engagement levels with their financial results. The companies with high employee engagement had a 19% increase in operating income and 28% growth in earnings per share. Conversely, companies with low levels of engagement saw operating income drop more than 32% and earnings per share decline 11%.

Chicago-based researcher ISR conducted a study among more than 664,000 employees in 71 companies worldwide and found that there was a difference of almost 52 percent in one-year performance improvement in operating income between companies with low employee engagement and companies with high employee engagement. The high-engagement organizations improved by 19.2 percent, while the operating income of the low-engagement organizations declined by 32.7 percent over the period of the study.

Gallup Management Journal's Employee Engagement Index reported that in the USA 17 percent of employees are positively disengaged, 54 percent of employees are not engaged, and a disappointing 29 percent are engaged. They estimated that the cost of disengaged employees was between $250 and $350 billion *per annum*.

What's clear is that organizations with high employee engagement are dramatically more successful than those with low employee engagement (not to mention actual disengagement) where it counts most – on the bottom line.

Employee engagement is essential for success in our challenging modern business environment – it's all about people.

One of the questions at the forefront of every results-oriented business leader's mind must therefore be: how do I develop higher levels of engagement in my people?

There are many measures of just what it is that creates an environment where employees are engaged in this manner, and almost as many programs for developing such an environment. Most are aimed at making direct changes in employees' environment and work conditions. This is all valuable, but it ignores an extremely important piece of this complex puzzle.

The Missing Link

What's frequently forgotten is the prime mover in creating an environment of engagement – the leader.

> *Fortune* magazine's "100 Best Companies to Work for" study revealed that an engaging workplace is driven by three interconnected relationships:
>
> - The relationship between employees and management.
> - The relationship between employees and their jobs/company.
> - The relationship between employees and other employees.

Let's look at those first two points. This is often overlooked: employee engagement, and all the positive business benefits it brings with it, is largely driven by those we put in charge – the managers and leaders at all levels of our organizations. Anyone who supervises or leads people has an enormous impact on engagement, for better or worse. From the first two points in the *Fortune* quotation it is clear that at least two-thirds of the responsibility for an engaging environment falls on the leader, and, of course, the influence of the leader can be critical in the third point.

This is the often-forgotten reality of employee engagement: if the leader is not creating an engaging environment, then, no matter what else you do, your people will not be engaged.

And this is where the concept of charisma in leaders starts to become very interesting indeed.

Leadership Charisma and Employee Engagement

Arthur C. Clarke famously said, "Any sufficiently advanced technology is indistinguishable from magic." It is a classic human tendency to describe anything we do not fully understand in magical or mystical terms.

The ancient Greeks observed that some people, generally their leaders, had what they perceived to be a mysterious quality that enthralled others and made them want to follow them. Because they didn't understand what this quality was, and because they couldn't quite pin it down, they decided that it must be a magical or God-given gift. They even created a special word for this mysterious attribute. They called it *kharisma* – "a divinely conferred gift or power" (www.dictionary.com).

That word from ancient Greece has found its way, largely unchanged, into many modern languages. In all of those languages you'll find definitions of charisma similar to the one the Greeks used several thousand years ago. In one modern dictionary charisma is defined as "a gift or power believed to be divinely bestowed" (Encarta Dictionary: encarta.msn.com).

If you look at some of the other dictionary definitions of charisma, however, it becomes obvious that there is more than a passing connection between charisma and employee engagement. Look at the definitions of employee engagement and charisma below. The observation of the closeness of these two definitions was the genesis of this book.

Employee engagement	Charisma
"... a heightened emotional connection that an employee feels for his or her organization, that influences him or her to exert greater discretionary effort to his or her work." (The Conference Board)	"... a special quality of leadership that captures the popular imagination and inspires allegiance and devotion." (www.yourdictionary.com)

What is abundantly clear is the direct connection between a leader's charisma and business results. Employee engagement drives business results; charismatic leaders bring people onboard, driving employee engagement. So focusing on becoming a more charismatic leader is a clear way to obtaining superior results from people.

Director of Research at the Rofley Park Institute, Jo Hennessy, put it perfectly: "Charismatic leaders can gather people behind them. They're inspiring and strong and, if they're able to engage staff, the results will follow."

The most dangerous leadership myth ... asserts that people simply either have certain charismatic qualities or not. That's nonsense; in fact, the opposite is true. Leaders are made rather than born.
— Warren Bennis, leadership scholar

You Can Be a Charismatic Leader

The reason that most people confer magical status on charisma is that they mistakenly think of it as an attribute that an individual possesses – and nothing could be further from the truth.

Charisma is not an attribute, but a perception one person has of another whose personality he or she finds appealing. No one can be charismatic on his or her own. It takes two people – one to observe what he or she describes as charisma, and another to behave in a manner that the observer perceives as being charismatic.

Charisma is truly like beauty – in the eye of the beholder. If I find you charismatic, then, for me at least, you are.

Charisma is simply the combination of the impact of a wide variety of behaviors that people observe practiced, consciously or unconsciously, by those they term charismatic.

Ask ten people to explain why they find someone charismatic and you'll probably get ten different answers. Some will talk about the person's ability to speak in an inspiring manner. Others will describe his or her genuine friendliness. Still more will talk about the interest he or she shows in other people's well-being. And others will mention many more things, which we'll explore later in this book.

And they would all be right – charisma is whatever others observe it to be.

Charisma is a term applied to us when someone likes the combination of how we behave, the actions we take, the face we present to the world, the words we use, our body language, and myriad other things. All of these contribute to a greater or lesser degree to our perceived charisma.

So charisma is not a particular quality that a person either possesses or doesn't possess; and it's based on behaviors, so it's definitely not something that is innate.

When you think of charisma in this manner then it becomes clear why some people are perceived as charismatic in one setting but not another. Someone who has developed superior oratory, presentation, and performance skills may come across as a charismatic speaker when addressing a group of hundreds of people, but be singularly uncharismatic immediately afterward when talking one on one with members of the audience – because of a lack of one-on-one social and communication skills. Similarly, someone may be charismatic for one group of people who finds his or her behaviors appealing and not at all charismatic to a group that does not.

Everything we do contributes to or detracts from our charisma. Those who are charismatic simply display more of the behaviors that promote a "charismatic response" in those others who matter to them. Some people do this quite effortlessly – there is something in their genes or in their upbringing that makes this the most natural thing in the world; the rest of us must learn how. And learn we can.

The good news is that, because charisma is based on behavior, it can be measured – and it can be cultivated. Anyone can decide to become more charismatic and, simply by assimilating the behaviors that will be deemed charismatic by his or her target audience, that person can raise his or her perceived charisma in pretty much any situation.

This is especially good news for business leaders, for whom charisma is an absolutely indispensable element of success in modern business.

If you wish to, you can become a genuinely charismatic leader.

Leadership Charisma: Two Core Principles

As we wrote this book we continually searched for any overriding principles that explained why people react charismatically to one person and not to another. We found that looking at things from the perspective of those perceiving charisma is very enlightening, and doing so provided us with two principles – "WIIFM?" and the "Charismatic Equation" – which will be extremely useful in helping you determine whether any planned action or behavior you might consider will have any charismatic impact upon those who work for you.

We mention both several times throughout the book to draw your attention to how two such simple ideas can be extraordinary predictors of what will be seen by others as charismatic behavior or charismatic leadership.

"What's in It for Me?" (WIIFM?)

This is not as cynical as it might sound, but when you strip away all of the niceties, all the layers of "proper" behavior that define the way we act and interact with others, all the social norms and so on, self-interest tends to inform most of what we do.

It's that simple. That's why the WIIFM acronym is one of the most recognizable in the lexicon of every English-speaking businessperson.

Before doing anything asked of them, even the most altruistic people, at least unconsciously, ask, "What's in it for me?" And if the answer is "nothing" then they generally don't do what's asked unless they're coerced into it.

Recognize that those who are charismatic are always appealing in some real way to the wants and needs of those upon whom they have a charismatic impact. They always answer the WIIFM question. Think of any situation where an individual is considered charismatic by any group of people and you'll see how she or he is, to some extent, giving them what they want or need at that point in time.

The Charismatic Equation

The Charismatic Equation describes how charismatic people meet a fundamental and universal human need in those they interact with – the need to feel positive about oneself and one's situation. The Charismatic Equation states simply:

> The extent to which you are perceived as being charismatic is directly proportional to the extent to which people either feel or fare better after each interaction with you.

Make a positive difference in the way people feel or in how well they do and they'll find you charismatic.

Our experience in researching this book showed us that almost anything a leader can do to have a charismatic impact on his or her people can be explained using one or both of these principles.

Observe how true this is as you work through the book. If you choose to take nothing else away from your read, take these two critical ideas into consideration every time you do something that will have an impact on those who work for you.

A Practical Model for Charisma in Business

When we set out to write this book our initial research had established that charisma was a function of others' perceptions of behavior, so we knew that any leader could choose to raise his or her perceived charisma simply by focusing on developing appropriate behaviors.

The studies that already existed on charisma in commercial environments certainly demonstrated that a leader's charisma inarguably plays a large role in driving the performance and productivity of his or her people. There is a large body of research that shows a direct connection between bottom-line results and leader charisma.

Having determined the intimate connection between employee engagement and the charisma of leaders, we set about an intensive research study of everything we could find that had ever been written on the topic of charisma. Our objective was simple – to construct a model of charisma that would facilitate both its practical measurement and its practical development in leaders.

An early result of this research was the realization of the key role self-confidence plays in a leader's charisma. Another result was our recognition of just how important a leader's "physical charisma" – that is, movements and body language – is in the projection of a charismatic image. This provided us with two of the critical steps in the Leadership Charisma Model introduced in Chapter 2.

Our initial version of this model was a great step forward, but it still did not achieve all we had set out to do. We still did not have the complete model needed to provide the basis for step-by-step development of charisma in any leader who desired it. We uncovered a lot of usable and credible research on charisma in general, and all of it completely backed up our belief that charisma was driven by behavior. It even helped to identify a number of the behaviors that drive the perception of charisma. However, much of the existing research was, in general, too vague or imprecise to allow for the development of a practical guide that would allow leaders to identify exactly what behaviors they must assimilate in order to increase their leadership charisma.

There was just too little usable research on *practical* approaches to developing charisma in business leaders.

Real-Life Charismatic Leaders

So we turned our attention to a wide variety of well-known business leaders who were globally acknowledged as charismatic leaders and who had had extraordinary business success.

We looked at everything we could find that they had written on leadership, and anything that had been written on their leadership styles, that would help to uncover what drove their charismatic impact on their people.

Among others, we studied the following leaders.

Larry Ellison, the billionaire founder of Oracle Corporation, has been a passionate and inspiring visionary for Oracle, and for the software industry at large, since he founded the company in 1977.

Steve Jobs is the chairman, CEO and co-founder of Apple Inc., makers of the Mac, iPod, iPhone, and iTunes, among other products. He is well known for his engaging and highly charismatic presentation style.

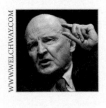

Just as well known for his larger-than-life personality as for his enormously successful Virgin Group, Richard Branson is a classic charismatic leader.

Jack Welch was CEO of General Electric for 20 years and is known as one of the most successful and charismatic business leaders of all time.

CHARLIE BREWER

Michael Dell founded Dell Computers in 1984. He grew that company into one of the most profitable computer companies in the world. His particular ability to communicate his engaging vision has been credited as central to his success.

ONINNOVATION

An engaging, charismatic, and hugely phil-anthropic leader, Pierre Omidyar is the founder and chairman of eBay, the online auction website that has revolutionized online commerce.

AMAZON.COM

A former *Time* magazine man of the year, Jeff Bezos is a celebrity entrepreneur known as much for his upbeat personality as for his commercial know-how. The company he founded, Amazon.com, is a global household name.

PROCTER & GAMBLE

A.G. Lafley retired from his position as CEO of Procter & Gamble in 2010. Lafley is credited with revolutionizing that company, increasing its market value by more than $100 billion.

GETTY IMAGES

George Zimmer is a household name in the US for personally advertising the company he founded, Men's Wearhouse. Zimmer is well known for his people-focused style of management.

SALESFORCE.COM

Marc Benioff founded Salesforce.com in 1999. A visionary who focuses on the people aspects of his organization, Benioff has made his company the leader in enterprise cloud-computing systems.

Meg Whitman is the fourth richest woman in California. She is best known as the former CEO and president of eBay. She left eBay in 2008 to try to become governor of California.

Highly charismatic entrepreneur Scott Cook co-founded Intuit Inc. in 1983 and now serves as chairman of its Executive Committee.

John Chambers is chairman and CEO of Cisco Systems, Inc. He has received numerous awards for his leadership over his past 14 years and has been included as one of *Time* magazine's "100 Most Influential People."

By the age of 40 David G. Neeleman had founded three successful low-cost airlines, the most famous of which being JetBlue Airways. JetBlue is known for its exceptionally high level of service.

From what had been written by, and about, these paragons of the art of charismatic leadership we found a great amount that clearly and definitively underlined the behavioral basis for such leadership. You'll find words from each of these leaders quoted throughout this book.

But while this did further underline that everything our research had told us to that point was borne out by real-life experience – that charisma was clearly driven by specific behaviors – it still did not give us a definitive snapshot of the key behaviors that drove leadership charisma. Without those we knew we couldn't build a practical model that anyone could use to develop his or her own charismatic appeal as a leader.

Brand New Research

If we wanted to complete our model we were left with just one option – to do all of the necessary research ourselves. This was obviously going to be a demanding and expensive exercise, but the temptation of uncovering such a model was just too much. And so we committed to taking on this huge project.

However, before we could do any research we had to define exactly what it was we wanted to find out.

Leadership Charisma – a Definition

Not wishing to add any further confusion to the already confused topic of "general" charisma, we decided that there was need for a new term for that particular type of charisma that all business leaders must aspire to. This kind of charisma includes all of the usual attributes associated with charisma, but also a focus on driving employee engagement and bottom-line results. The term we settled on was "leadership charisma."

We defined what charismatic leaders did as follows:

> Charismatic leaders create and maintain a work environment where people are emotionally and intellectually committed to the organization's goals. They build an energetic and positive attitude in others and inspire them to do their very best. In doing so they create a common sense of purpose where people are more inclined to invest extra energy and even some of their own time in their work.

That's leadership charisma.

With a clear definition of leadership charisma and its impact on business performance, we were ready to undertake what we believe to be the largest global study ever undertaken on the topic of what behaviors drive this quality.

That research is detailed in Appendix I. The results you'll read about there allowed us to build the Leadership Charisma Model we introduce in Chapter 2.

The Leadership Charisma Model

Charismatic leaders create and maintain a work environment where people are emotionally and intellectually committed to the organization's goals. They build an energetic and positive attitude in others and inspire them to do their very best. In doing so they create a common sense of purpose in which people are more inclined to invest extra energy and even some of their own time in their work.

W E SET THE objective of writing a book that would provide a comprehensive model of leadership charisma, allowing any leader to take a step-by-step approach to developing the sort of charismatic leadership that gets extraordinary results from people. We succeeded.

Remember, when we set out to create the Leadership Charisma Model we had three rich sources of information at our disposal:

- Our own research – the largest study ever undertaken, we believe, to find the specific behaviors that generate leadership charisma.
- Our analysis of all of the previous research we uncovered on charisma (particularly in leadership situations).
- The insight we had drawn from our research into highly successful and world-renowned charismatic leaders.

We blended all three information sources into a single model, imposing a logical structure on leadership charisma. The result was the four-step/layer Leadership Charisma Model introduced in Figure 1 below.

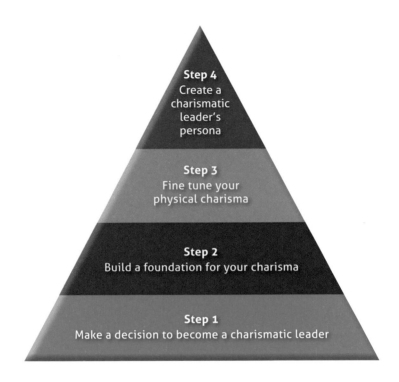

Figure 1: Leadership Charisma Model.

This model presents a systematic four-step process for developing robust leadership charisma. What follows is an overview of each of those steps.

Step 1: Make a Decision to Become a Charismatic Leader

As you've already seen Chapter 1, charisma is all about behavior. If you wish to become a charismatic leader, then you must make the decision to assimilate the behaviors that typify charismatic leaders. Step 1 concerns that critical decision.

Step 2: Build a Foundation for Your Charisma

The Leadership Charisma Model is in the form of a pyramid – one of the most stable structures known to mankind. The pyramids in Egypt are believed to have stood for more than 4,000 years and to have settled by no more than a few inches in all of that time.

Why? Because the foundations are outstanding. And even though you cannot see those foundations (they are buried below the surface) you can certainly see the beneficial effects of having such a firm base. The foundations made the pyramids sustainable in the very long term.

From our research into charisma in business environments, and from simple observation of individuals widely acknowledged as charismatic business leaders, it became obvious that a critical component in charisma is solid self-confidence. It is quite simply impossible to build a sustainable charismatic persona until you have developed a stable foundation of self-confidence. Just like the foundations for the pyramids, self-confidence is largely invisible – but it makes your charismatic persona sustainable in the long term.

Step 2 is entirely devoted to helping you build this critical foundation layer. Even if you feel yourself to be supremely self-confident, we strongly recommend that you take some time to review this section. It covers critical issues like the role of clear personal goals and provides an insight into critical tools and techniques for creating a single-minded focus on those goals. A critical element in self-confidence is a clear sense of purpose and forward motion.

This section also introduces the Haney-Sirbasku Success System – a simple system you can use to focus yourself on achieving your goals and building your self-confidence in just 15 minutes a day.

Step 2 will help you build a solid foundation of self-confidence that will make your charisma much more natural and sustainable.

Step 3: Fine Tune Your Physical Charisma

As you work through this book you'll find that there many facets to the jewel that is charisma. A crucial and highly visible facet, and one you can start working on right away, is your "physical charisma."

We spent a lot of time looking at video footage of those acknowledged as charismatic leaders. What was obvious was that charismatic people share a number of physical behaviors. The way they carry themselves, the way they smile, the manner in which they look at those they're talking to, how they gesture, and the extent to which they touch others all communicate an enormous number of charismatic messages.

Step 3 looks at the critical role your body language plays in the propagation of a charismatic persona. It takes you step by step through the physical behaviors you can start to apply right away to raise your charismatic impact on others.

If you begin to make the physical behaviors outlined in Step 3 part of your everyday body language, you'll find that people respond to you in a dramatically different way.

Step 4: Create a Charismatic Leader's Persona

Step 4 takes our own substantial research, everything we learned about charismatic leader behaviors from our review of all existing research, and all we gleaned from observing established charismatic business leaders, and blends them into a single step-by-step, behavior-by-behavior program for developing a charismatic leader's persona.

Charismatic leaders are characterized by enormous energy and enthusiasm, and by irrepressible and highly attractive optimism.

By knowing their industry and fields of expertise better than anyone else they can develop clear visions of what they wish to achieve. They work hard to share the passion and hunger they have for that vision with those around them.

They communicate every message, however small, with passion and energy, and they are keenly aware of the pivotal role that communication plays in the perception of charisma.

By focusing on bringing out the very best in others and making others feel positive about themselves and successful in what they're doing, they inspire everyone they come in contact with.

Their clear expertise, compelling visions, and other-person-focused attitudes are positively infectious and make them decidedly attractive to anyone they interact with.

Step 4 looks at practical ways in which you can harness all of the critical attitudes and the associated behaviors typical of charismatic people to drive your own charismatic impact through the roof.

Raising Your Leadership Charisma: Getting the Most from This Book

Each of the four steps in this model has multiple chapters associated with it, and each chapter covers a single separate aspect of leadership charisma. Figure 2 provides an overview of the chapters under each step.

Figure 2: Leadership Charisma Model, chapter by chapter.

Here's what we suggest is the best way to get maximum results from the leadership-charisma-development program we present in this book:

1. **Jump right in**

    In thinking about the best way to advise you on getting the best from this book we all agreed that we didn't know too many people who, when reading a book like this, would pick it up and read it cover to cover – without knowing what was coming and whether the journey was going to be worthwhile. So the first thing we suggest you do is follow your inclination to bounce through the book's sections and chapters in whatever order appeals to you. We have written each chapter so that it can be read in isolation. Each chapter delivers great ideas and value, even if you never read another, and each can be read in as little as 10–15 minutes.

2. **Start to apply some of the ideas**

    One of the great things about charisma is that it is behaviorally oriented and multifaceted – so you can build your charismatic leadership style step by step, one behavior at a time. So, as you jump around reading chapters the way we suggest, be sure to start to apply some the ideas you're reading about to your daily business life. Apply any one idea for a week or two and you'll start to see how it has some small impact on the people who work for you and around you. With each chapter, you'll learn something of immediate practical value and get great ideas – even if you never get around to reading the entire book. All of the chapters have been written so that they can stand completely alone if need be. However, the way to get the best long-term return on your investment in this book is, of course, to read it in its entirety.

3. **Harness the ripple effect**

When you drop a stone into a pool the impact creates ripples that spread out from the point of contact. They weaken a little as they get further from the point of impact, but, as you no doubt have observed, even a small stone can create ripples that will be felt right across the full width of a large pool.

That's the effect you have when you take one or other of these leadership-charisma behaviors and start to apply it in isolation as discussed in Step 2. You will see some impact, which is better than nothing, but it won't be significant. If you take a handful of those behaviors and begin to apply them in an unstructured manner, it's like throwing a succession of small stones into your pool. Each time you toss one in you'll get ripples, and the more you toss in the more ripples you'll get. But it really doesn't matter how often you throw those small stones into the pool – you'll never really get any greater impact.

What if, instead, you took all of those small stones and invested the effort to bind them together into a larger mass? What would happen when you tossed that into your pool? The impact would be much greater. The amplitude of the ripples would increase dramatically; the ripples would travel a lot farther and have a much bigger impact on the far side of the pool. And, of course, the more small stones you compress into your larger mass, the bigger the impact you'll have.

This book provides you with an insight into all of the various individual behaviors that have a charismatic impact on others. More importantly, it also provides a step-by-step approach to putting those various behaviors together in a systematic way. This will help you build a charismatic persona that will be much more impactful and sustainable in the long term than if you simply applied the behaviors at random.

If you take the approach of working through this book one step at a time, and working through the Leadership Charisma Model layer by layer, then at the end you'll enjoy much greater success in applying what you learn. You'll see your charismatic impact grow stronger and more sustainable as you apply the lessons from each successive chapter.

Taking this more systematic approach will also result in more of those behaviors becoming a completely natural part of the way you behave from day to day – so that charisma becomes a natural by-product of the way you conduct yourself.

That journey starts with Step 1 – with the critical decision to become a charismatic leader.

Step 1

Make a Decision to Become a Charismatic Leader

Step 4
Create a
charismatic
leader's
persona

Step 3
Fine tune your
physical charisma

Step 2
Build a foundation for your charisma

Step 1
Make a decision to become a charismatic leader

Decide to Be a Charismatic Leader – and Commit

FROM CHAPTER 1 it is obvious that charismatic leaders are much more likely to engage their people, with all of the research showing clearly that this engagement positively impacts their organizations where it matters – on the bottom line. So all leaders with a focus on the bottom line should also be focused on raising their charisma.

From our research, with what we believe is the largest study ever undertaken into what drives leadership charisma, it has become equally obvious that leadership charisma is in no way magical – it is simply a question of behavior. Leaders who are perceived to be charismatic are those who behave charismatically. It really is as simple as that.

In Stephen Covey's excellent book *The 8th Habit: From Effectiveness to Greatness,* he observes:

> Inspirational leaders choose to be inspirational leaders – they make the choices
> that enable them to become inspirational leaders.

It's the same with charismatic leaders. All you need to do to become a charismatic leader is decide that you wish to be one – and then choose to develop those behaviors that will make you charismatic.

Becoming a charismatic leader begins with this critical first step – the decision to commit to the development of behaviors that will drive your leadership charisma higher and bring you the results achieved only by those charismatic leaders who inspire their people to greater levels of engagement and productivity.

The most important word in that point is "commit." In one of his very entertaining keynote speeches Zig Ziglar said that "most people are about as committed as a kamikaze pilot on his twenty-ninth mission." So true. That's why most people are not charismatic. Becoming charismatic requires a commitment to invest the time and energy to learn how to be charismatic as well as dedication to putting that knowledge to work consistently.

Most people will not make that investment. If you are prepared to do so then you can become one of those charismatic leaders who touch everyone they meet, who achieve extraordinary results for their organizations, and who enjoy highly successful careers as a result. If you follow the four steps in this book we guarantee that you will become more charismatic than you ever thought possible.

If you've just made a commitment to doing that, then you've already completed the first step on this journey. You're now ready to move forward to Step 2, in which you will build a firm foundation for your charisma.

Step 2
Build a Foundation for Your Charisma

Step 4
Create a
charismatic
leader's
persona

Step 3
Fine tune your
physical charisma

Step 2
Build a foundation for your charisma

Step 1
Make a decision to become a charismatic leader

Have you ever met a charismatic person who lacked self-confidence, seemed anxious, or was obviously unduly stressed or worried? No, of course not! One of the things that makes a person charismatic is the fact that he or she does not outwardly display these all-too-common human frailties.

Charismatic people always seem centered, confident and calm. If you can keep your head while all around are losing theirs, then you're on the road to charisma.

Self-Confidence – the Foundation of Charisma

Much of the behavior we display to the outside world is a reflection of the inner world we all occupy and live in from day to day – the world inside our heads where our likes, dislikes, attitudes, moods, and beliefs about ourselves rule our every thought and, in turn, many of our outer behaviors.

There are many inner factors that foster a successful development of sustained charisma, but none is more important than self-confidence.

Why Does Self-Confidence Elicit a Charismatic Response?

The answer is simple: because we all aspire to be more self-confident, we always find self-confidence attractive in others.

Next time you're in the company of someone who appears supremely confident, take note of the effect it has on you. You'll find that you automatically straighten yourself up and begin to act more confidently. You tune in to her or him. This is the effect you have on others when you behave confidently. Self-confidence is more contagious than any disease. It jumps from host to host in the blink of an eye.

Most people, regardless of the masks that they wear, are much less self-confident than they appear. If another person makes them immediately feel and act more confidently, then that person instantly becomes more charismatically attractive. Many people harbor an unconscious hope that, if they associate with self-confident people, some of that confidence might just rub off onto themselves. For this reason anyone who has developed superior self-confidence is immediately attractive to others.

Self-Confidence Is Critical

It really does not matter what else you do in the pursuit of charisma if you're not self-confident. No one will be charismatically affected by someone who is unsure of himself or herself, nervous or fumbling. If you want to have a sustainable long-term charismatic impact you must start by making your self-confidence absolutely bulletproof.

When you look at the most successful people you see that success breeds confidence, confidence drives success, and success in turn breeds even more confidence. It's the original "virtuous circle." To get that whole wonderful cycle started you need a good starting point – a solid foundation for self-confidence.

And that starting point is the establishment of a structure that ensures that at any moment in time you are always automatically focused on spending your time, energy, and effort on those activities that will get you the results you desire and make you successful.

Self-confidence is all about attitude. If you decide to be self-confident and take the appropriate actions then you will become self-confident. If you're already quite confident you can always become even more so. You need no one but yourself to build self-confidence; it starts and ends with you.

General Electric's charismatic former CEO, Jack Welch, for example, has nominated self-confidence as one of the keys to a leader's success in motivating people to great results.

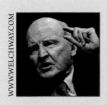

WWW.WELCHWAY.COM

Insecure managers create complexity. People must have the self-confidence to be clear, precise, to be sure that every person in their organization – highest to lowest – understands what the business is trying to achieve.

— Jack Welch, former chairman and CEO, General Electric

There are lots of people who are extremely competent but not confident – because they have not yet given themselves permission to be confident. Confidence begins to build when you decide that you will allow it to do so. Decide to do that now.

Step 2 provides four chapters that will help you build absolutely bulletproof self-confidence:

- **Chapter 3: Live in the Present**
  When you have the sense that everything that you are doing at any point is time is taking you exactly where you want and need to go, then you know that your future success is assured and you become naturally self-confident. The first chapter in this step, "Live in the Present," talks about the critical role that setting and achieving meaningful goals plays in developing the sort of robust self-confidence that is at the heart of sustainable charisma.

- **Chapter 4: Visualize Your Success**
  This chapter takes you step by step through harnessing your visualization capabilities to ensure that you achieve your goals and develop a deep-rooted sense of self-confidence, which you transmit from deep inside you to the outside world.

- **Chapter 5: Control Your Mind**
  In "Control Your Mind" we show you how to tune out those annoying negative voices inside your head that nibble away at your self-confidence and get in the way of success – especially at times of stress or pressure.

- **Chapter 6: The Haney-Sirbasku Success System**
  Bud Haney and the late Jim Sirbasku created a systematic way of pulling the ideas and techniques outlined in Chapters 3, 4, and 5 into a single system for managing a successful goal-focused life. This system assures your success and builds the self-confidence that is key to charisma, and it takes only about 15 minutes daily to apply. This chapter takes you through creating your own Haney-Sirbasku Success System.

As we mentioned above, simply behaving charismatically will produce a charismatic reaction in others, which in turn will raise your self-confidence. But that's the slower way to go about things. Doesn't it make much more sense to make developing solid self-confidence a priority? Doesn't it make sense to accelerate the process of building a solid foundation on which to construct your charismatic persona?

Put that foundation in place now with Chapters 3 to 6.

REACH GOAL!

STICK TO IT

GET TO WORK

MAKE PLAN

- SET GOAL

S ELF-CONFIDENCE IS CRITICAL if you wish to become charismatic – and nothing eats away at self-confidence more than the sense that time is passing and nothing is being achieved. It is critical that at any given point in time you feel you are doing everything you should be doing to assure your success.

Now Is All You Have

When we were researching this book we came across an absolutely fascinating way of looking at the passage of time. According to Google, the same piece of writing appears on about 2,000 separate pages worldwide, but we couldn't find out who originated it.

Imagine you had a bank account where, just after midnight every night, an installment of $86,400 was credited. The only problem with the account is that you are not allowed to carry over the balance from day to day – and any outstanding balance is cleared from the account just before midnight every night.

You cannot draw out the balance and save it elsewhere because it's not allowed. What would you do? I'm guessing that you'd figure out a way to invest every cent of that $86,400 every day, in the way that would give you the best possible enjoyment and return.

We all have such an account – with the Bank of Time. Every day we're given 86,400 seconds and we get to decide what to do with them – to invest them wisely or to let them slip by unused.

Any time you let go by is gone forever, and you cannot draw against the future. All you have is the present moment.

As the saying goes:

Yesterday is history,
Tomorrow's a mystery;
All we really have is today.
(Anon)

There's another version of this thoughtful saying:

Yesterday is history,
Tomorrow's a mystery;
Today is a gift – which is why it's called the present.
(Anon)

Goals Plant You Firmly in the "Now"

The reality is that all you ever have is the present moment. That's where you always live – never in the past and never in the future – so all of your efforts should be on ensuring that you use the present moment as productively as possible. You should also seek to make the present moment as habitable and pleasant as possible, and make sure that coming present moments (that is, the future) are equally pleasant places to be.

Goals are an essential element of self-confidence because they make you feel strong and assured about the here and now. They give you the faith to take control of the current moment and live it with gusto. Clear and compelling goals provide you with a confident clarity as to what you should be doing right now. They provide direction and the focus that makes it possible to choose what action to take at any given time. They make it possible to prioritize. If you have clear goals, you must invest all of your present moments so that they produce a future return on investment.

In his early twenties Ted Turner (the charismatic founder of CNN) started working full time in his father's billboard advertising business. His father, Ed Turner, grew up during the Great Depression and Ed's parents lost almost everything during that period. This hardened Ed Turner's resolve and he set the goal that he would one day own a plantation and a yacht. By the time Ted Turner joined the business, his father had achieved all that. Ted recalls him saying:

> Son, you be sure to set your goals so high that you cannot accomplish them in
> one lifetime. That way you'll always have something ahead of you. I made the
> mistake of setting my goals too low and now I'm having a hard time coming up
> with new ones.

Clear and challenging goals allow you to forget the future, which doesn't exist anywhere except in your imagination, and live fully in the present, investing yourself completely in the best life you can make for yourself. Compelling goals are the motivational fuel that lights you up with self confidence – and makes you a beacon that continually and automatically focuses on behaviors that are compellingly charismatic.

Making Goals Work for You

Creating a set of goals that put you firmly on the road to success, and shore up the self-confidence that is the essential foundation for charisma, takes a little time and energy. But the payback is enormous.

Here's a six-step approach to creating great confidence-building goals.

1. **Have goals for all aspects of your life**
   To be effective at keeping you on positive self-confident ground in the present moment it is essential that you not confine your goal-setting to business. To be entirely confident of everything you're doing now you

need to be sure that you have all aspects of your life covered.

At a minimum we suggest you create goals in at least the following five areas of your life:

- Career and business.
- Relationships and family.
- Financial.
- Health.
- Personal development.

And don't forget to make one of those career and business goals that you will become a charismatic leader!

2. **Write them down**

The very act of committing goals to paper allows you to visualize more clearly exactly what it is you wish to achieve. While they are in your head they are abstract ideas, but the moment you put pen to paper you make them much more concrete. Your goals become much more real to you.

Don't settle for the first draft. Write them and rewrite them until they really resonate with you and get you excited. Be sure that they are clear and specific. This has the very positive effect of priming your mind, sending it the clear signal that this is something you're serious about. In research by Gail Matthews of Dominican University, those who wrote their goals down "*accomplished significantly more* than those who did not write their goals" (emphasis by the author).

3. **Create "word pictures" for each of your goals**

All three of us are graduates of the Dale Carnegie program. One of the things that stuck out in all of our memories from that program was the way that Carnegie instructors suggested we should write goals.

They suggested creating "word pictures" for our goals. Written goals become word pictures when you use language that would make anyone reading it get a clear and compelling picture of exactly what this achievement means to you. Word pictures are not the sort of dry descriptions written for a report. Instead, they should be excited, elated, positive descriptions that light up the image of each goal in your mind.

To get started, Carnegie instructors always recommended that goal word pictures should begin firmly in the present tense with "It is … [a future date]," and "I am … [where you are]." You must write the descriptions as if you have already achieved the goal in question.

The goal word picture should go into as much detail as possible on how the achievement of the goal has affected your life – how it feels to have achieved it, how it is affecting you and those around you, and the positive changes it has made for you and your loved ones.

Take a look at the example we have included in Appendix II. In that example we have blended a series of goals together into a compelling word picture for a set of goals that have a one-year focus. Your word pictures should have this same positive, upbeat and motivating tone, and should focus on a holistic improvement that covers all areas of your life and business.

4. **Create a mixture of large, medium-sized, and small goals**

The great thing about having goals for all aspects of your life is that it gives you enormous scope for having a good mixture of goals of varying size, impact, and timescale. Why? Because there is nothing quite as confidence-affirming as achieving a goal. Work it out so that you have a continuous stream of small, medium, and large goal victories. Every day should bring the achievement of some goal or other, however small. And every day should bring the satisfaction of moving larger goals closer to achievement.

5. **Don't delude yourself that setting a goal is enough – create milestones**
   Once you've made each goal, plan out some of the actions you'll take to achieve it. Set up milestones for each that allow you to nibble away at them all on a daily, weekly, and monthly basis.

The Acid Test of a Goal

And here's the acid test when you've sketched out a goal. Does it really fire you up? Does it make you excited to be alive, filling you with a motivation to take on the world right this very second? If not, then trash it – it's not for you.

Your goals should make you positively glow with enthusiasm, energy, and excitement about your opportunities. If they do then they are working. Not only will they make your life a much more exciting place to be, but the energy and enthusiasm that they create in you will be instantly perceptible to all others around you. That halo of self-confidence comes from deep inside of you but can be detected by all around you in the way you walk, talk, and behave. It is at the very core of charisma. The confidence that comes from having really compelling goals sets on autopilot several behaviors that we'll discuss later in this book – behaviors that will kick-start your charismatic appeal.

AMAZON.COM

A lot of people ... believe you should live for the now. I think what you do is think about the great expanse of time ahead of you and try to make sure that you're planning for that in a way that's going to leave you ultimately satisfied. This is the way it works for me.
— Jeff Bezos, founder, Amazon.com

Bud Haney always suggests you ask yourself: "What can I do today that I did not do yesterday – that will make tomorrow better?"

There is so much more we could say about goal setting, but this is not purely a goal-setting book. There are plenty of fine examples of those easily available. One book that takes a really interesting approach to creating compelling goals, and one which we'd recommend, is *The Answer* by John Assaraf and Murray Smith. Not only do the authors write extremely well on the subject of goal setting, but they have also become serial entrepreneurs and multimillionaire successes as a result of applying the techniques they write about.

Visualize Your Success

Just creating a set of positive goals gives such a sense of purpose, provides such a clear direction for everything you do in the present, and creates in you such a sense of optimism about the future that you cannot help but be more self-confident. That self-confidence will be sensed by all of those around you as the beginnings of charisma.

With your goals defined, you can start to build your self-confidence – and your charisma – even further by bringing those goals to a successful conclusion. That success starts the first time you create a clear picture of what achieving those goals would do for you.

Chapter 4, "Visualize Your Success," takes the next step in building a foundation of self-confidence for the charismatic personality you are setting out to develop.

Visualize
Your Success

4

I N THE INTRODUCTION to Step 2 we established the key role that self-confidence plays in charisma. Without robust self-confidence it is pretty much impossible to sustain a strong charismatic demeanor.

In the last chapter you saw that one of the most effective ways to build your self-confidence is to establish and achieve goals in all parts of your life.

Think about your most challenging goals. How confident would you feel if you had achieved all of those goals? How would it impact on your self-confidence, and therefore your charisma, if you found that everything you turned your hand to worked out well – and every day brought the completion of another of your goals? Stop for a moment and just try to imagine it.

Wouldn't your self-confidence soar? Wouldn't you feel like you could do pretty much anything? You can easily see how the self-confidence you'd exude would positively light up those around you with a charismatic glow.

Well, you don't have to wait until you reach your goals to gain that unbeatable self-confidence and to feel that way.

Your Amazing Brain

There are two things everyone should know about the way the human brain operates:

1. Your brain doesn't know the difference between real and imagined events.

2. Your subconscious mind is always on autopilot – in a powerful search mode that you program.

1. **Your brain doesn't know the difference between real and imagined events**

   Your brain is a wondrous organ that retains a memory of every real-life experience you have ever had. It also retains a memory of any experience you have ever imagined. The interesting thing is that it cannot differentiate between events that have really happened and those that you only imagined. So, when you vividly imagine an event, your brain experiences that event in the same way as a real happening – and it has exactly the same neurological effect on you as a real-life event.

   If your brain were a man-made machine we might consider this to be a shortcoming, but for our purposes it opens up some extraordinary possibilities for dramatically raising both your self-confidence and your ability to hit your goals.

2. **Your subconscious mind is always on autopilot – in a powerful search mode that you program**

   Have you ever been in a busy place like an airport where there's lots of noise, hundreds of simultaneous conversations going on and lots of noisy announcements coming from all around you? Suddenly a single voice cuts through all of the background noise and grabs your attention, tuning out everything else. Perhaps you hear someone speak your name, or you hear the easily recognizable voice of a friend; perhaps you just hear someone speaking with an accent similar to yours. Either way, it cuts through all of the chaos to grab your attention.

   That's your Reticular Activating System (RAS) in action.

   Your RAS is like a conduit between your conscious and subconscious mind. It takes orders from your conscious mind and relays them to your subconscious – orders like, "Listen for my name," or, "Listen out for anyone I know." The RAS takes its orders from your thoughts and the images they conjure up. Everything you think about is fed to the RAS.

You can think of your RAS as a waiter. Thoughts passed to the RAS are like an order to the kitchen of your mind for what you'd like to see served up on the table of your life.

So when you dwell on the potentially negative outcomes of a situation, you create a vivid picture of those situations in your mind. That picture is passed to your subconscious, with the order that the RAS should seek opportunities to make it come to pass. You become subconsciously focused on what you fear most.

Of course, you can use the RAS to your advantage – by denying it any negative or catastrophic images and instead feeding it a diet of positive images of what you positively *do* want. Visualizing the successful achievement of your goals programs your RAS to scan your environment continuously for anything that will help you make that achievement possible.

Through regular visualization your RAS can be programmed to continuously seek out opportunities to bring your goals to fruition faster.

Once programmed, the RAS works away quietly in the background, doing all it can to identify opportunities to make whatever you ordered a reality. This personal search engine is continuously scanning your environment for what you've indicated is of interest to you.

Now let's put what you know about your amazing brain to positive use and help you to achieve your goals, raise your self-confidence, and make yourself more charismatic.

Your Current Programming

Your perception of who you are, your view of yourself, your attitudes and your beliefs, and your perception of your strengths and weaknesses have all been built inside your brain, piece by piece, over years. Everything your brain has experienced, real or imagined, has had an impact on making you who you are today. It is this inner image of yourself that determines how you react to the situations you meet daily. It directly impacts your mood and the thoughts you think; it determines how you react to the situations you encounter every day, and it drives your everyday behavior.

If your self-image is positive and self-confident then your outer behaviors will reflect this. You will mirror on the outside what you see and feel on the inside. If your inner image of yourself is less positive and robust than you'd like, this too will be reflected in your normal outer behavior and demeanor.

Over time this interpretation of yourself becomes stronger and more fixed and less likely to change. As you are exposed to more and more experiences your brain tends to interpret everything you encounter in a way that fits with and reinforces this well-established image of yourself. Events are interpreted in such a way that they fit your current beliefs about yourself and the world around you.

Unfortunately, if these life experiences have programmed your self-image with any limitations (e.g., poor ability to communicate, inability to inspire or lead people, lack of charisma, challenges in managing your finances) then everything that happens to you continually reinforces those self-imposed limitations.

This means that, unless you make a conscious decision to change your "programming," you'll get more of the same from life as time goes on. As the saying goes, "Keep doing what you're doing and you'll keep getting what you're getting."

Now, here's the good news: you can harness the brain's inability to tell the difference between real and imagined experiences to completely reprogram your internal view of yourself.

You Are Visual by Nature

"Seeing is believing." "If I hadn't seen it with my own eyes I wouldn't have believed it." You've heard both of these exclamations a thousand times, right? Somehow, when you can actually see something it becomes much more real, much more credible. It becomes entirely believable.

By your very nature you are visual. We all are. Look at the success of the multimillion-dollar movie industry; look at TV. We all respond much more strongly to visual imagery than to any other stimulus the world feeds us.

Consider your thoughts. Are they more like a series of words or a succession of images – small movies or TV programs playing one after another in your head? You think in images – it is the most natural thing in the world for you.

You built your entire view of who and what you are through your thoughts, through inner visualizations, and you can use the same process to change that view.

Visualization

Once you've created a compelling set of meaningful goals for every part of your life, you can use those goals to radically overhaul your internal image through a simple process of visualization. If your brain cannot tell the difference between real and imagined experiences, real and imagined successes, then doesn't it make sense to feed it a diet of successful experiences that will build a stronger, more self-confident view of yourself? It's like tricking your brain into believing you've enjoyed much more success than you have – with all the benefits of the self-confidence that goes along with such success.

I train myself mentally with visualization. The morning of a tournament, before I put my feet on the floor, I visualize myself making perfect runs with emphasis on technique, all the way through to what my personal best is in practice ... The more you work with this type of visualization, especially when you do it on a day-to-day basis, you'll actually begin to feel your muscles contracting at the appropriate times.

— Camille Duvall, professional waterskier

Even sportspeople like Camille Duvall, the "Golden Goddess" of waterskiing, use visualization as an integral part of their training regimes.

As soon as you visualize your goals, you take the first step in making them very real, believable, and achievable to you. As soon as you can "see" the successful completion of a goal, you can start to see the way to get from where you are now to that end point.

One of Bud Haney's favorite sayings is, "Visualize things as they can become – not as they are." Visualize your goals as if they have already been achieved and you have directed your RAS to find every possible opportunity to make this so. Your goals come alive inside your brain in such a way that you can conceive of no outcome except the one you desire – and you start to think and act accordingly.

> If you have multiple goals for multiple aspects of a well-rounded life, and if you take the trouble to visualize them regularly, the impact on your self-confidence will be enormous. You will see yourself become everything you ever wanted to in all aspects of your life.

At its most basic and accessible, visualization is simply a mechanism that keeps a clear and compelling picture of what you want to focus on right in front of you from day to day.

This is why writers create outlines, movie producers produce storyboards, and architects produce three-dimensional models – it helps them to focus on what they want to produce. Without this ability to visualize the end product, books would not be written, movies wouldn't be made, buildings wouldn't be constructed.

Visualization promotes a clear focus, which means that you more easily make the right choices, prioritizing the right actions as you go about your day-to-day business. That sense of purpose and self-assurance generates self-confidence.

Visualizing Versus Dreaming

You already visualize – all day, every day. Every time you think through a challenging issue you find yourself visualizing the various potential solutions and imagining the potential outcomes. Visualization is as natural for humans as walking upright. That's why it's a little strange to notice how many businesspeople are immediately turned off when you start to talk about using visualization as a means of achieving goals.

For some people visualization sounds just a little too much like self-delusion, aimless daydreaming, or an exercise in pure naive hope – none of which is a worthwhile investment.

Let's be clear. If all you do is visualize, then you're a dreamer. If, however, your visualization creates a clear, compelling picture of where you want to be and what you want to achieve, and suggests actions you can take to further your goals, then it is nothing put positive. If focused, positive visualization makes you so self-confident that you go after your goals with enthusiasm and energy, does it make any sense not to use this simple success tool? Of course not!

With a pattern of visualization formally structured into your daily routine you can harness any spare mental bandwidth that might otherwise be occupied with worries or negativity. You'll find you solve problems and bounce back from setbacks much more quickly and feel down an awful lot less.

How to Visualize

Some people like to sit down in a quiet place and close their eyes to visualize their goals; some people even like to enter a light meditative state to tune out distractions and allow the mind to focus on the visualization fully. It's really compelling to have your visualizations read to you, in your own voice, while you're in a relaxed state.

But you don't have to close your eyes for visualization to be effective.

If the eyes-closed meditative approach is not for you, then all you need do is choose a place where you'll get 10 or 15 minutes completely to yourself. Select somewhere you feel comfortable and relaxed – somewhere that goes some way to cutting you off from the cares of your day.

Then simply read slowly and thoughtfully through the word pictures you created for each of your goals. Don't hurry through this reading; instead, take the time to savor every word and to really experience consciously how it feels to have achieved the goal. Read it as if the goals have already been achieved. Take a few moments to imagine how it would affect you and all of those around you, how you would feel.

The real beauty of visualization is that it is not at all complicated. You are already a natural visualizer; you use this capacity unconsciously every day of your life. Now you're going to consciously harness it in the service of your success.

A little later, in Chapter 6, we introduce Bud Haney and Jim Sirbasku's own tried and tested visualization system – a single, compelling, daily "eyes-open" technique that is fast, effective, and easy to integrate into a busy day.

When I get a new idea, I start at once building it up in my imagination, and make improvements and operate the device in my mind. When I have gone so far as to embody everything in my invention, every possible improvement I can think of, and when I see no fault anywhere, I put into concrete form the final product of my brain.

— Nikola Tesla, inventor of radio and the electric motor

Create a Daily Visualization Routine

It is good to have a routine whereby you do your primary visualization exercises at the same time every day. Select a formal time and location – this makes it more likely you'll take time out to reinforce your visualizations daily. Experiment with a few different times of day and find which one works best for you. The aim is to create a quiet window where you are not distracted.

Establishing a routine like this is important to ensure that you make visualization a standard part of your everyday life. As you do so you'll find that things become much clearer for you. Your priorities will be unambiguous, and you'll constantly feel that whatever you're doing is making the best use of your time at that particular moment. Your self-confidence will increase dramatically and you'll find your optimism at a higher level than ever. You'll have a clarity of vision that lifts your spirit and your energy level unbelievably.

Ironically, it's at this point – when you're getting the most benefit from the visualization process – that you're most likely to drop the practice. You'll feel so good that you might easily decide there's no great need to keep it up. After all, you have great clarity already, right?

If you don't establish a routine you'll find that your daily practice falls off gradually to a point where it's entirely forgotten. And when it does, all of the benefits you've realized will begin to slip slowly away. Your mind will fall back into reinforcing the older self-image you've started to deconstruct – taking you back to where you started. Don't let that happen. Routine keeps you focused and ensures you build an ever more robust, positive, and motivating self-image.

Recycle Downtime

The visualization investment you'll need to firmly establish a goal in your mind will be determined by the goal's scope, its potential impact and the time it will take to achieve.

If you're working on a whole variety of goals of all sizes, impacts and timescales, then even a few moments as you walk through the airport to board your plane, or as you walk from office to office, can be enough to briefly visualize one of your smaller goals.

You may need a little more time to visualize medium- and longer-term goals completely. For those goals you can recycle time that might be otherwise be downtime. Taking the bus or train or walking to and from work is a prime example. The almost hypnotic effect of taking a journey you take hundreds of times a year and you could probably do blindfolded can create the sort of receptive mental state that makes it easy to visualize the successful outcome of your goals – rehearsing your success in full living color. A recording of your own voice reading through your goal word pictures can assist with this greatly.

Post-Visualization Reminders

Jim Sirbasku always counseled having Post-it notes or other reminders with goals written on them placed in strategic places where you are likely to be when the opportunity to recycle some time occurs.

Putting brief reminders anywhere they might be seen, even momentarily, to make you think about one or more of your goals is a positive addition to any goal-visualization strategy. A Post-it note on your shaving or make-up mirror, a brief list of key goals attached to the dashboard of your car with Velcro, a revolving series of reminders in the screensaver or wallpaper of your computer, or even a brief note in your wallet can be helpful in re-priming your RAS with some of your key goals.

Visualization Builds Self-Confidence and Focus

Visualization is a powerful way to build unshakable self-confidence.

In the opening to this chapter you briefly imagined what it would be like if all of your goals had come to pass – how that would bolster your self-confidence. Now, with visualization, every day you can tap into the self-confidence, optimism, and energy that comes from such success.

As soon as you have a clear, compelling picture of what you're trying to achieve, it suddenly seems so much more possible. Every time you create a vivid image of the successful completion of a goal, your mind believes you have scored yet another success. It raises your mood, lifts your thoughts into more positive territory and enhances your self-confidence. This positions you even more strongly to get the success you're striving for.

But just as importantly, that self-confidence is absolutely radiant, raising your charismatic appeal to those around you.

Controlling Your Mind

Through visualization you are harnessing one of the most powerful capabilities you have and creating a great foundation of self-confidence on which you'll build a more charismatic persona.

Be warned, however. As you do so you may find that you encounter a little opposition from your conscious mind – which may resist the messages from your visualizations. You'll see how to deal with that in Chapter 5.

Control
Your Mind

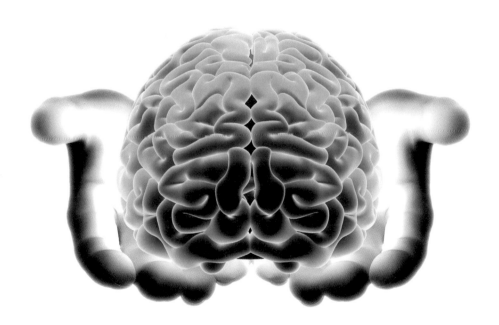

S o you've built an inspiring set of goals and started to use the power of daily visualization to focus yourself daily on their achievement. As you visualize your goals (as if already completed) to sow their seeds in your subconscious, you may find that your conscious mind jumps in and starts trying to derail you. It's almost like there's a voice inside your head saying, "Hey, you should know yourself better – you'll never achieve that! Forget it!" or, "No, you haven't achieved that yet!" That's just your "self-talk." It's normal and it can be managed.

Have you ever castigated yourself when you did something wrong, or failed at something – especially something simple? Have you sometimes said something like "Oh, that is just typical of me," "I am so dim sometimes!" or "I always screw up at that!"? Admit it. We all have – and you hear people do it all around you every day. Sometimes the outburst is in your head; sometimes it's out loud.

> You talk to yourself continuously. There is a continuous dialog running inside your head. What you tell yourself drives your thoughts, your feelings and much of your day-to-day behavior. It determines in large part your mood from moment to moment and the way you react to the circumstances around you. So it is critical that you direct your self-talk so that it is positive and supports the goals you're pursuing.

Eliminating negative self-talk and replacing it with positive self-talk is a priority for those wishing to consistently achieve their goals, raise their self-confidence and create a charismatic persona.

First, Rid Yourself of Negative Self-Talk

Left unchecked, negative self-talk reinforces a negative image of yourself and your performance.

In his book, *The Silva Mind Control Method*, José Silva provides a simple and highly effective way of diminishing the impact of negative self-talk on self-confidence and optimism. Next time you catch yourself saying something negative, cancel the effect of the thought. Just say "Cancel, cancel," to yourself, and tell yourself that doing so will erase the negative impact of the thought or self-talk. This is a great exercise in pulling yourself up and beginning to gradually eliminate your negative self-talk as and when it happens, breaking the habit.

You need nothing more complicated to deprive negative self-talk of its impact on you. Make this simple practice the norm any time you doubt yourself or begin to dwell on negative self-talk.

As you eliminate your negative self-talk in this manner, you need to replace it with some positive self-talk. And you do that with affirmations.

What Are Affirmations?

Affirmations are simply positive statements designed to change your self-talk to an entirely positive dialog over time.

Practicing affirmations is simple – you simply establish statements that describe *the beliefs you'd like to have about yourself* and begin to recite those statements to yourself on a regular basis. Over time your self-talk begins to center on these new messages and becomes more accustomed to being positive in nature, allowing no space for more negative thoughts.

At their most basic, affirmations are simply a system for reminding yourself who you want to be and what is important to you. Remember your Reticular

Activating System (RAS) from Chapter 4? If you keep a model of your ideal self to the front of your mind, you're simply priming your RAS and continually reminding yourself to be on the lookout for opportunities to develop and reinforce that ideal self. An affirmation does not have to be an accurate statement of how you feel about yourself now. It should be a specific statement of *how you wish to be*.

Creating Affirmations

To create your affirmations, start by understanding that your aim is to create a complete picture of how you want to think about yourself and what you wish to become – in a series of simple statements.

There are some important guidelines for creating effective affirmations.

- **Use the first person singular in the present tense – "I am …" and "I can …"**
  The idea that you already have those qualities you aspire to makes the statement more immediately believable to your subconscious mind, which, as we saw earlier, does not know this is a statement of fact. Your mind programs you to behave as if you already are what your affirmation tells it you are. Phrase your affirmations to address how you'd like to be in this present moment.
- **They must be positive**
  Your brain can easily visualize positive situations and outcomes, but it cannot easily tell the difference between positive and negative statements. Have you ever played a game where you are about to take an important shot and you say to yourself,

"Whatever you do, don't miss!" What inevitably happens? You miss! What your brain processes is, "Whatever you do ... miss!" and it promptly sets up to do what you've programmed it to. So, don't use affirmations like "I am not overweight" or "I do not lack self-confidence." Instead, phrase them positively: "I am my perfect weight." "I am completely self-confident."

- **Keep them short, sweet and to the point**
  This makes them easy to remember and easy for your mind to process.

- **Use language that touches you emotionally**
  If just repeating the affirmation to yourself as you write it gets you thinking, "I wish!" then it's right. If it evokes no longing or positive emotional response in you, rewrite it.

- **Write them down, then rewrite them**
  When you have written your affirmations down, repeat them to yourself a few times. You'll find you need to fine tune them to get them feeling like they fit you. Keep refining them until they evoke an excited and positive response in you. Over time you'll find yourself fine tuning them again and again, adding new ones in to counteract negative beliefs and self-talk patterns you recognize.

Some Affirmation Examples

Here are a few examples of affirmations to get you thinking as you begin to develop your own personalized affirmations.

To Become Generally More Charismatic

As you work through this book you will develop your own affirmations to specifically target those parts of your self-talk that may be stunting your charismatic appeal or general success. In the meantime, these are a great starting point for anyone wishing to become generally more charismatic.

- I am a charismatic person.
- My self confidence, enthusiasm, and energy shine through in everything I do.
- I am friendly, approachable, and genuinely interested in others.
- I am a great listener.
- I am a powerful and compelling speaker.

To Be a More Charismatic Leader

In later chapters you'll see how these affirmations go right to the heart of a leader's charisma.

- I inspire all of my people to be their very best.
- I make a positive difference in every interaction with my team.
- I always look for the potential in my people.
- I am interested in helping my employees succeed personally.
- I am indispensable to my team, which views me as a positive source of inspiration and guidance.
- I help all of my people become everything they possibly can.
- I am a role model for all of my team.

To Become More Positive

If you tend toward a less optimistic outlook, it can diminish your charisma. This set will help to promote a more positive outlook and will enhance your self-confidence and positivity.

- I am positive and confident, and I approach all situations with a determined, can-do attitude.
- I am optimistic and always find a way to respond positively to challenges.
- I control my feelings and always choose to be positive.
- I feel great about myself.
- I have incredible potential.
- I believe in myself totally.
- I am completely confident.
- I am successful in everything I do.

To Worry Less

Aimless worry affects your thoughts, your mood, and the face you present to the world. Worried people are not charismatic people. Replace worry with positive action and you sap its paralyzing effect.

- I never let worry paralyze me: I always take positive action in the face of problems.
- I have no time for groundless fears, and even when I feel justified fear I take the right action, which dissipates that fear completely.
- I am totally unafraid to say what has to be said and do what has to be done in order to be happy, content, and successful.

These may be a useful starting point for drafting your own affirmations, but the key to success lies in crafting your own affirmations. They must be motivating and energizing for you.

Become aware of your self-talk and identify any negative beliefs about yourself that may be holding you back. When you identify such a belief, create an affirmation to cancel it out. If it's particularly acute, create a few different affirmations so that you come at it from different angles.

If you need more inspiration, go to an Internet search engine and enter "affirmations." You'll find tens of thousands of sample affirmations that will give you inspiration for creating your own.

When you have created your own suite of affirmations, the next step is putting them to work.

Using Your Affirmations

It's critical that you take control of your self-talk, eliminating all negative self-talk and replacing it with empowering, positive self-talk. Begin to talk to yourself more positively in terms of how you'd like to be and you'll find yourself beginning to act as if that's how you already are.

If you want to become more charismatic you need to begin modeling that new charismatic self-talk inside – and then allow it to filter out into your everyday behaviors.

That's where affirmations are absolutely key to charisma. If you don't see yourself as confident, successful, and charismatic on the inside, anything you do to become charismatic on the outside will feel, and look, fake.

By consistently using your affirmations you feed your mind a continual diet of positive thoughts, which positively impact your emotions. They in turn impact the way you go about things on a daily basis.

Affirmations are effective only if you use them, repeating them to yourself on a regular basis. If you repeat your affirmations daily they become second nature to you. They supplant alternative and less palatable negative thoughts and beliefs that can cause damage to your self-confidence, energy, motivation, and mood.

I know that you're probably extremely busy, but you cannot leave these affirmations to chance, hoping you'll use them on a regular basis. It makes much more sense to create a routine to ensure that you take time to repeat them to yourself at least once daily.

The Haney-Sirbasku Success System pulls together your goals, visualizations, and affirmations into a single, easy-to-use, eyes-open process that will allow you to create positive habits that make sure you are always focused on your goals and always working on your self-talk. For maximum impact, why not combine both approaches?

You can read about how to do so using the Haney-Sirbasku Success System in Chapter 6.

The Haney-Sirbasku Success System

> The vision must be followed by the venture. It is not enough to stare up the steps, we must step up the stairs.
>
> — Vance Havner, preacher

Vance Havner nails the challenge to any busy leader. Even when you know precisely what you should be doing, it can still be a challenge to get started doing everything you need to do.

With Chapters 3 to 5 complete, you have three-quarters of the foundation layer of the Leadership Charisma Model covered. You know that in order to create that critical base of self-confidence on which you'll build your more charismatic persona, you need to formulate a set of whole-life goals, then harness the tools of visualization and affirmations to keep you focused.

Sounds easy – until you consider everything else you have to do, right?

This is a challenge that the three authors of this book took on and defeated many years ago with the creation of a simple system that you can now adopt. The Haney-Sirbasku System makes it easy to blend all three of these foundational items into your busy day – for a daily investment of just 15 or 20 minutes.

Bud Haney and Jim Sirbasku revolutionized the modern employee-assessment industry. Profiles International, the company they founded in 1991 with a modest stake of just $25,000, now has more than 1,000 business partners in more than 100 countries worldwide, servicing 45,000 clients in every conceivable industry.

The Haney-Sirbasku Success System has been at the core of the work Bud and Jim have done to develop the organization over the last 20 years and is very much responsible for the success of Profiles International.

The System

The system is straightforward. First, buy yourself a good-quality three-ring binder. Set up six dividers and populate each section as follows.

- **Accomplishments**

  In this section, write down details of anything notable you have ever achieved – especially goals that you set and realized. Don't forget things like testimonials, press clippings, and anything else that reminds you of times when you performed at your best and that makes you feel generally good about yourself.

  Celebrate your strengths and successes. It does not matter who you are or what point you're at in your life or career. We can guarantee that you have forgotten more of your achievements than you remember. It's human nature: we ditch our achievements and focus on what we still have not yet achieved. We all need to remind ourselves of just how successful we already really are.

  When someone congratulates you on a speech or on a particular job well done, make it a habit to ask that person if he or she wouldn't mind writing down some comments. Some will, some won't. But every personal testimonial like this will further reinforce your self-confidence. Build all of those into this section.

- **Current goals**

  These are goals that have target deadlines somewhere in the next six months, so you'll probably be working on them or thinking about them often. It's essential that you keep these goals in front of you every day.

- **Medium-term goals**

  "Medium-term" means different things to different people. We define it as being in the six-month to two-year timeframe. These are goals that you will probably be working on a little less frequently but that need some attention nonetheless so they progress toward completion.

- **Long-term goals**

  In this section go goals that stretch somewhere beyond the two-year vista, perhaps even many years into the future. These goals are long term.

- **Dreams**

  Earlier, in the section on visualization, we cautioned against daydreaming. This is something completely different. These are goals that seem so far beyond where you are now, so outside what you see yourself as capable of achieving in the timeframes above, that you do not want to assign timeframes to them.

  They are things you'd like to achieve at some point in your life – things that you will move into the long-term-goals section when the means for progressing them becomes clearer to you.

- **Affirmations**

  Earlier you saw how to create affirmations that would build your mental fitness and eliminate any negative self-talk. Your affirmations go in this section. All of the research on this topic shows that key constituents in the success of all high achievers are the positive messages they feed themselves daily.

Apart from the personalized affirmations you developed for yourself earlier, you might be interested in two of our favorite "off-the-shelf" affirmations. The first is based on one written by motivational speaker Zig Ziglar, who suggests a strong affirmation:

"I love myself, I love what I do, and I will be successful in the short, medium and long term." The second is from Émile Coué, a French psychologist who died in 1926. It is wonderful in its simplicity: "Every day, in every way, I am getting better and better."

Affirmations are a key element in this system. At the very least, harness those written by Zig and Émile.

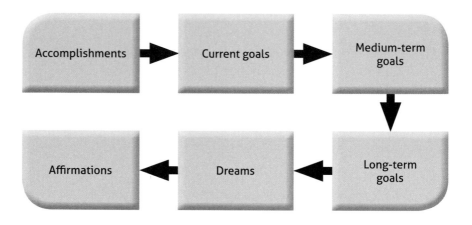

Figure 3: The Haney-Sirbasku Success System – 15 minutes a day.

Using the System

Having populated your binder, the approach for working through the Haney-Sirbasku System really couldn't be simpler. All you need do is review this binder *every* day, reading through each page in order – from front to back.

The way you review it is important too.

Read through each section thoughtfully in the order indicated in Figure 3. Start with the "Accomplishments" section and work from there. Savor each word and briefly visualize what each sentence means for you. This sounds easy, but it can be quite a challenge. After four or five days you'll be so familiar with the content that you may be inclined to speed read – to rush through some of the sections.

Accomplishments

The first section, "Accomplishments," is a case in point. You are entirely familiar with the content of this section – so much so that you'll be inclined to take it for granted and sweep through it quickly. Don't!

It is important that you read through this section deliberately. Carefully reminding yourself of all of your accomplishments will help shake off the negative impact of the inevitable setbacks that will confront you during your working day. Think of the impact of a daily reinforcement of all you have achieved to date. Think about how that sets you up for a productive and positive day.

Current Goals

Next comes the "Current Goals" section. This is key because there may well be some action you can take today to further or even complete these goals. Just reading your goals again like this brings them to the front of your mind, reprogramming your brain's RAS to be on the lookout for anything that comes your way during the day that might help you further those goals.

This simple eyes-open visualization of your goals sets your conscious and subconscious mind on full alert for opportunities to further what you're aiming to achieve.

As you work through this section, a day will come when a goal has been achieved. Put a line through that goal and allow yourself to enjoy the satisfaction of that achievement. Don't rewrite your list. There is a very positive motivational value in seeing a page that has some completed goals already crossed out. If you continually rewrite the page so that all you have is a perfect list that never seems to get any shorter, you can create a sense of being a hamster on an exercise wheel – going around and around but never quite getting anywhere. Leave the evidence of your progress in place.

When you cross that goal out decide to celebrate it in some way during your day. Depending on the magnitude of the goal the celebration may be as little as a treat with your coffee or as much as a week or two in the Cayman Islands. Celebrate your achieved goals.

Medium/Long-Term Goals

Now read through your section on medium-term goals. Again, be sure not to rush through them. Focus on them enough to create a visual image of what it will be like to have achieved each goal. On some days you will realize that a medium-term goal has moved forward enough to become a short-term goal. This is another success. You have moved a larger goal closer to completion. Draw a line through that goal and transcribe it into your "Current Goals" section. This is an important ritual. The crossed-out goal in your medium-term section will be a positive fillip for you every day you read that section from this point forward. It will remind you of your continual progress.

Do exactly the same with the next section on long-term goals.

Reviewing your long-term and medium-term goals just as much as your current goals is a critical element in the success you'll enjoy with this system. Long-term goals become medium-term goals when you spot opportunities to bring them closer to completion; medium-term goals become short-term goals, and so on.

Opportunities to move these forward will often pop up unexpectedly and may go unrecognized unless your goals are clearly drawn in your mind. Reading through these sections reminds you of your priorities – of why you're doing everything you're doing – and reassures you of your ongoing progress.

Goals Can Become Stale

Circumstances change. People change. With such changes some goals can go out of date. They can lose relevance and become stale.

Sometimes, however, when you've had a goal in front of you for a while and have invested some time and energy in its completion, you can be reluctant to ditch it regardless of its relevance. Quite naturally, you do not want to waste your investment to date.

Remember the approach we suggested earlier for screening whether or not a goal is worthy of your attention? If, upon working through your system, you should find that any of these goals no longer lights you up with enthusiasm, no longer makes you long for its achievement, then it's time to lose it.

> The most important value of a goal is its ability to motivate and excite you to new levels of energy and optimism today. If any one of your goals no longer does this, then it will have no value to you when you achieve it. Drop it right away – it is not doing its job. Put a line through it.

Clearing unworthy goals in this manner is a triumph too. You've created even greater clarity and focus for those goals that *are* worthy of you.

You Can See Your Progress

As you work through your system over time your goals will progress from "Dreams" to "Long-term," from "Long-term" to "Medium-term," from "Medium-term" to "Current." As they move from section to section you have an ever-more-inspirational record of your progress – each goal's journey through your system is entirely visual – and you see it at the start of each and every day. The system itself is a powerful exercise in the visualization of your success.

Affirmations

So, you've reviewed your success and triumphs in full living color. You've reminded yourself of and visualized your current, medium-term, and long-term goals. You've set yourself up for a great day. Now, to put the icing on the cake, send yourself out into the world on a diet of affirmations that kill any negative self-talk and reassure you of your ability to recreate your previous triumphs and to achieve the goals you have set for yourself. Starting your working day with positives sets you up to make the most of each day.

When to Use the System

Many members of the senior team of Profiles International have applied this simple system over the years since Bud and Jim first shared it with us. There's no magic and no gimmick involved. But it does work – simply because it makes you think every day about the things that are important to you. This routine puts your conscious and subconscious minds on full alert for opportunities to help you move your goals forward. But better than that, particularly on tougher days, just having this system in place gives you a daily sense that you are continually moving onward and upward. It is motivating, energizing, and confidence building.

Bud suggests that your review of your system, which will not typically take any more than 15 minutes, should ideally be undertaken first thing in your working day. If you make it a ritual to work through your system before you do anything else each day, you start every day in the most positive and focused manner possible. There will be times when it won't be practical to get it in first thing, but be sure to do it at some stage during the day. Daily reinforcement is critical.

Give it a Test Drive

Establish this process as a habit. Maxwell Maltz, father of Psycho-Cybernetics, observed from his research that establishing a new habit takes 21 days. Why not give it a try for the next 21 days?

One thing we absolutely guarantee: use this system for 21 days and your self-confidence and optimism will soar – and with soaring self-confidence comes increased charisma.

Completing Your Foundation

With the establishment of your Haney-Sirbasku System you pull together the key constituents introduced in the introduction to this section as critical elements in building robust self-confidence. The self-confidence that comes from knowing that you have a compelling set of goals for all areas of your life, from living these goals daily through your visualizations, and from the constant diet of positive self-talk your affirmations provide to your mind, will rocket your self-confidence.

Even if you start out quite self-confident, getting this level of control over your life will cause your confidence to soar. As your self-confidence soars, so will your charisma – and there is nothing more attractive.

Use the Haney-Sirbasku System daily and Step 2 will take care of itself, continually strengthening the self-confident foundation for your charismatic persona.

With that process underway, you are ready to start looking at Step 3 – the development of your physical charisma.

Step 3
Fine Tune Your Physical Charisma

Step 4
Create a charismatic leader's persona

Step 3
Fine tune your physical charisma

Step 2
Build a foundation for your charisma

Step 1
Make a decision to become a charismatic leader

> The minute you walked in the joint
> I could see you were a man of distinction, a real big spender ...
> — Shirley MacLaine, actress, in *Sweet Charity*

T HE LYRICS OF that old Shirley MacLaine number capture an experience that most of us have had at some time in our lives – someone walks into the room and the entire room responds. Everyone's attention is drawn to the newcomer – for some reason no one can quite pinpoint.

There are people who have an immediate impact and radiate a physically charismatic appeal that draws people's attention to them. It's not necessary that they be celebrities or even known to others to have this impact. There is just something about these people that captures the attention of all around them. If that something can be identified, it can be harnessed.

Given that this impact frequently occurs before that person has even spoken, it is obvious that whatever is having this charismatic effect is entirely nonverbal. Instead, it is a collective impact of nonverbal cues that communicate a charismatic message as the person moves through the gathering with ease.

Physical attractiveness and sharp dressing help, of course. An attractive person will catch your eye more readily than someone less so. Someone who is particularly well dressed will also have this effect. The attractive and attractively dressed have a small head-start in that their arrival in a crowded room will naturally be noticed more. That's the simple nature of attractiveness.

But that's fleeting. Once someone attractive has been observed and examined, and perhaps even commented on, the conversation carries on as before – unless there's a little bit more there to pique the watcher's interest. Someone charismatic holds your attention for much longer. Your eye is drawn to him or her almost magnetically again and again, usually for no reason you can easily identify. What the charismatic person has obviously goes beyond simple attractiveness – so that even someone patently physically unattractive can have this impact.

If it's not just how these people look, not how they're dressed, and not what they say that is so charismatic, then the only thing it can be is their body language. All of this impact must be communicated by a combination of all of the subtle nonverbal messages that charismatic people's faces and bodies transmit.

Charisma Research: The Body-Language Connection

Researchers as far back as Darwin have pointed out the importance of nonverbal communication in the relationships between people.

Despite this fact little research had been done on this topic until relatively recently.

Howard Friedman is a psychology professor at the University of California – Riverside who has done extensive research on the part that body language and nonverbal cues play in our perception of charisma.

He describes charisma as a "certain presence" that gives an individual an aura of self-confidence, assurance, and a generally self-assured demeanor. According to Friedman, charismatic people are "generally popular because of their ability to transmit emotions through nonverbal cues."

Through extensive research he has demonstrated that charisma is directly proportional to the use of nonverbal cues or body language and can be measured directly though an examination of things such as facial expressions, body movements, gestures, and smiling.

According to Friedman's research, charismatic people tend to smile more than the average, with a distinct crinkling around the eyes demonstrating the genuine nature of the smile. They tend to use a lot of hand gestures and to touch people more when talking with them.

In the course of his research Friedman determined that "much of what is meant by charisma can be understood in terms of (emotional) expressiveness" (the ability to use body language to communicate nonverbally). Friedman developed the Affective Communication Test (ACT), which measures emotional expressiveness by observing a variety of nonverbal cues, including the extent to which people touch during conversations, are facially expressive, laugh heartily, and express emotions.

The ACT examines thirteen cues in all. All of the indicators Friedman uses to measure charisma are completely nonverbal and the test specifically measures the effectiveness with which people transit emotions to others using body language.

The ACT has been proved scientifically reliable and has been used effectively in large corporations for assessing leader and manager charisma.

Charismatics Transmit Their Moods to Others Wordlessly

In a fascinating study, Friedman showed just how dramatic an impact emotionally expressive/charismatic people can have on those around them.

He first identified two groups of candidates. One group was highly expressive and had scored highly in the ACT; the other was unexpressive, scoring dramatically lower.

Each of them was first asked to complete a brief questionnaire designed to gauge their mood at the start of the experiment. Then two of the low scorers were placed facing one of the high scorers for just two minutes. They were told that they could look at one another, but that they could not speak at all.

After two minutes each of the candidates was again asked to complete a questionnaire to determine their mood at that later point in time.

The findings were astounding. If, at the start of the exercise, the high scorers had described themselves as happy and upbeat, then at the end of the two minutes the low scorers also described themselves as more happy and upbeat (regardless of their moods before the experiment began). If the high scorers started out down and depressed, then at the end of the two minutes the low scorers also described themselves as being more down and depressed (again regardless of their moods before the experiment began).

The low scorers had "caught" the mood of their more charismatic peers. The only conclusion was that the nonverbal cues of the more expressive candidates – their facial expressions and general body language – had been communicative enough to wordlessly infect the low scorers with their moods.

In none of the experiments did the reverse occur. In no circumstances did the low scorers transmit their mood to the high scorers.

Friedman's experiments demonstrate the importance of nonverbal communication in developing charisma. This ability to infect another person with one's emotions was clearly one of the reasons that the ancient Greeks we mentioned in Chapter 1 described charisma as a God-given gift. Before research like Friedman's one could be forgiven for thinking it was all somewhat magical.

But now we know that there is nothing mystical about it whatsoever – now we understand the role that nonverbal cues play in communication – the implications are profound for anyone who chooses to focus on the development of his or her body language and other nonverbal cues. Not only can leaders who master their body language control the impression that others form of them in interactions, creating a more charismatic impact, but they can also directly transmit enthusiasm, energy, motivation, and even mood to those around them – without even saying a word.

BusinessWeek columnist Carmine Gallo describes the way the charismatic chairman and CEO of Cisco Systems John Chambers harnesses this powerful medium of communication:

> He touches people on the shoulder. He looks people in the eye. He gestures. Chambers's body language is authoritative, confident, and in control. Chambers makes sure the power of his movement matches the power of his words.

Think of the most successful and motivating speakers you have ever seen; think of the most charismatic people in our society. Consciously or unconsciously, they have harnessed their body language so that their presence alone is a strong message that has a powerful impact on those around them. Their message is being transmitted to others around by their simple presence. They do not even have to open their mouths to affect the mood in a group of people.

That truly is charisma in the raw.

The Body Language of Charisma

So the power of body language has been well established by modern science. What it makes clear is that our faces and bodies are like huge neon signs that continually transmit quite detailed information to those around us about our level of self-confidence, energy level, motivation, enthusiasm, mood, personality, and so on.

All of us have learned to be very effective readers of these nonverbal cues – even if we often do not even consciously realize that we are doing so. But not all of us have learned how to harness our nonverbal expressiveness equally well.

To become more physically charismatic it is obvious that you need to become more aware both of your current habitual body language and of the body language that has been proved to communicate a charismatic message.

To improve your physical charismatic impact on others there are some aspects of your body language to which you need pay greater attention, with a view to fine tuning them.

In Step 3 there are five chapters on body language that look at the nonverbal cues that have the greatest impact on your charismatic appeal:

● Chapter 7: The Charismatic First Impression
● Chapter 8: The Charismatic Smile
● Chapter 9: The Eyes Have It
● Chapter 10: The Charismatic Impact of Touch
● Chapter 11: Charismatic Gestures

And it all starts with the advice your mom gave you as far back as you can remember: "Stand up straight!"

The
Charismatic
irst Impression

7

YOUR MOTHER PROBABLY told you, "Keep your chin up," or your father may have said, "Hold your head high" – great advice if you want to make a strong, charismatic first impression.

As you approach someone, even from a such distance that they cannot see your face or make any other determination about you whatsoever, there is one aspect of your body language that still transmits a huge amount of information about you to all around – your posture.

Good, upright posture communicates self-confidence, energy, youthfulness, discipline, and strength. It says clearly: "I am entirely confident of myself and I expect you to respond accordingly." Poor, slumped posture communicates insecurity, poor self-image, lack of self-confidence, and a beaten demeanor, and has an extraordinarily negative impact on others.

You will never see any able-bodied person who is considered charismatic slumped or stooped.

To become more physically charismatic it is critical that you learn how to draw yourself up to your full height and adopt a self-confident posture.

Building a Perfect Posture

Your posture is good if, looking side on, you could draw an absolutely straight line from the middle of your ankle up through the center of your hip and shoulder, through your ear, and straight out the top of your head. The further you are from that straight line, the poorer your posture and the weaker the impact it makes on others.

Strip to your underwear and stand side on to a mirror. Don't look yet. Relax and assume your normal posture. When you've done so, turn your head and look for that line running from the top of your head through your ear, down through the middle of your shoulder blades, through the center of your hips and on down through your feet. Does your posture depart from that line? In what areas? Is your head forward or are your shoulders slumped to any extent?

Remember how your normal posture looked. Now stand with your back to a wall and your head held gently back against the wall as if you were being measured. Holding that posture, step away from the wall and back to the mirror – again, side on. Holding that pose, examine yourself again for that imaginary line. If you are looking taller or straighter now than with your normal posture, then you have some work to do in order to pull yourself up to your full height and create a positive and charismatic posture.

Many advise simply trying to hold the posture you get when you stand against the wall as we advised above. In our experience, though, it's not just difficult but downright uncomfortable to do so, and it makes for a fairly stiff and unnatural-looking posture.

There's a "trick" that models learn to help them present a perfect posture – one that works equally well for males and females and has the merit of creating a perfect posture without the robotic look of a back and neck held unnaturally stiffly from the shoulders up.

> Imagine you have a cable wired into your abdomen just a few inches below your belly button. Now, when you walk, imagine that someone is pulling you forward steadily with that cable – so that your hips are leading the rest of your body when you walk. The impact will be immediate. Your shoulder blades will raise and settle back into a positive posture with your eyes looking straight ahead. You'll also be quite relaxed in this posture.

If you use this simple visualization then you simply cannot stoop. It's impossible to slouch when you're leading the rest of your body with your hips. Over a short time, and with some conscious application, this will become second nature and the muscles that support a good posture will develop to make it entirely comfortable and natural.

What you'll notice almost right away is that this improved posture not only looks better but feels better too. There is no doubt that the solid self-confidence you built in Step 2 will be reflected in your posture – but the opposite is also true. Your improved posture will immediately enhance your self-confidence. You'll feel more confident right away. Try it – the view is really good from up there!

For the first few days you'll need to keep reminding yourself to do this every time you notice you have fallen back into your previous posture, but over time it will become second nature.

Exercise

As you start to raise your head into a more upright position it is now being carried entirely on top of your neck and shoulders. At about 8 percent of your body mass, and typically 3–4 kilograms or 6–8 pounds, this is quite a weight. For the first few days you do this you may find that you're employing the muscles in your upper body in a way you've never done before.

So expect some stiffness and soreness until the muscles adapt. You can offset this by getting your local gym to recommend some exercises and stretches to strengthen your neck, shoulders, and core. Those exercises, if performed correctly, will also tend to draw you into a better posture and make it comfortable for you to maintain a good posture naturally all day long.

Your Walking Pace

Every move you make has a positive, neutral, or negative impact on your charismatic appearance. To maximize the positive message transmitted when you walk, pay some attention to the way you walk – especially your pace. This means moving quickly, but without looking rushed. Moving too quickly or too erratically can create a harried or confused appearance. You are definitely moving too quickly if your speed causes you to lose control of your posture, for example. Similarly, walking too slowly can look lazy, uncertain, and lacking in confidence. Walk with purpose, maintaining your good posture all the time. Walk like you know exactly where you're going, and like nothing will stop you from getting there.

Once you hit the right pace you'll know it. You'll feel comfortable, energized, and self-confident, and you'll find it easy to maintain your best, most charismatic posture.

Seated Posture

Your seated posture is no less important a part of your charismatic impact on others than your standing and walking posture – especially if you spend any of your time in seated meetings. You cannot allow your posture to collapse just because you've sat down.

With so many of us spending so much time in front of PCs it is no wonder that seated posture is more of a challenge today than it has ever been. Quite apart from the benefits of avoiding neck and back pain, a good seated posture is also essential to the communication of a self-confident, charismatic message.

However, note that there is a difference between the posture that is good for your back and the posture that sends a charismatic message in a meeting.

Seated Working Posture

In a normal working situation your PC should be at eye level so that you need only move your eyes to see the entire screen comfortably.

Sit with your behind pushed right back in your chair and your lower back well supported (use a lumbar support if necessary), and then move the chair to a distance from the keyboard such that your hands can reach it, your wrists are straight, and your back and shoulders are straight and supported by the chair. Your desk should be approximately at the level of your belly button, and your elbows should fall slightly below the level of the desk. Tilt the seat forward so that your knees are lower than your hips by 20–40 degrees.

This will keep your head, neck, and back from suffering unduly when you spend a long time sitting, ensuring that you do not suffer posture problems as a result of a lot of sedentary work. However, this is not the seated posture that will have the charismatic impression you want in a meeting situation.

Seated Charismatic Posture

In a meeting situation, sit more to the front of your seat, with your back straight, feet planted firmly on the floor, and lean forward slightly. Sitting forward with your back straight in this manner brings you up to your full seated height and provides a seated version of the posture you developed earlier for standing and walking. As you'll see in a later chapter, leaning in slightly like this conveys eagerness, energy, and interest.

First Impressions Last

Frequently, the first impression you make on others comes directly from your posture, so it's important that you fine tune this critical nonverbal cue, so that you consistently send a message of energy, engagement, interest, and self-confidence – a core charismatic impression.

Once you have your posture under control, and a positive first impression is assured, you can start to work on the nonverbal cue that is almost as effective at long range as your posture – your charismatic smile.

The
Charismatic
Smile

8

ONCE SOMEONE HAS taken in your excellent posture and is sufficiently attracted and interested to look a little closer, what's the next thing that person's eye is drawn to? Your face, of course. We all unconsciously know that our faces are wired directly into the emotional centers of the brain and that our facial expressions tell those around us a lot more than almost any other communication method, verbal or nonverbal.

When you meet someone, the first thing you tune into is his or her smile – or the lack of a smile if none is on display.

Smiling is the universal human indicator of acceptance. Even in remote tribes where there has been no exposure to the world at large, researchers inevitably find that the smile is the most positive facial expression human beings can display.

A warm smile conveys friendliness, openness, confidence, optimism, and even a sense of fun. A smile is a positive recognition of another person, a way of reaching out that dissipates fear and reduces defensiveness. There is no doubt that the extent to which we smile is a universal determinant of our likeability.

[T]he expression one wears on one's face is far more important than the clothes one wears on one's back.

— Dale Carnegie, author and lecturer

Positive Effects of Smiling

Traditionally we tend to think of our facial expressions as a simple outward expression of the emotions that are roiling inside our minds. That's correct – but it's not the whole story. What recent research has shown is that our facial expressions also directly affect our mood and even play a part in determining the emotions we feel inside. Facial expressions are wired into the left frontal cortex of the brain – the area in which happiness is registered. When you adopt a positive, smiling expression, the feedback from your face to your cortex triggers the release of the neurotransmitters serotonin and dopamine into your brain. These are "feel-good" chemicals that have the effect of improving your mood. Smiling has even been shown to trigger the release of oxytocin, the so-called "caring hormone," which leads to greater bonding and intimacy.

There is now an enormous body of research outlining the positive physical effects of smiling. They include:

- Raising your mood and making you more positive.
- Boosting your immune system.
- Reducing your blood pressure.
- Increasing your self-confidence.
- Making you younger looking and more attractive to others!

According to MD Cliff Kuhn, "Within our personal chemistry we carry a medicine that reduces stress and prevents depression even more effectively than any pill ... the medicine of humor." According to Kuhn, many of the positive effects of smiling are possible even from fake or "social" smiles.

Duchenne Smiles vs Social Smiles

Believe it or not, this is not new knowledge. Charles Darwin was the first to observe that the physical changes caused by an emotion – like smiles or frowns – as opposed to being simply the consequences of that emotion, actually had a direct impact on it. So, your emotions affect your facial expressions, but your facial expressions also affect your emotions. If you don't like your current mood, then you can begin to change it by changing your facial expressions, the smile being the most powerful tool for doing so.

Guillaume Duchenne was a French neurologist who died in 1875. His research into smiling was the foundation of much of today's research – but it remained unexamined and undeveloped until relatively recently.

He is best remembered for the two main types of smile he identified:

- **The Duchenne smile**
  This is where two muscle groups of the face are engaged. One raises the corners of the mouth, and one raises the cheeks and forms "crow's feet" around the eyes – the classic crinkling we observe in someone displaying what we perceive as a "genuine" or "heartfelt" smile.

- **The non-Duchenne smile**
  This is where just one group of muscles is used – to raise the corners of the mouth. This is what we'll refer to as a "social smile" – a smile one adopts purely for social reasons, which is devoid of genuine emotion. The eyes remain totally unengaged.

While some researchers suggest that even an affected smile – what Kuhn refers to as a "fake smile" and what we call a "social smile" – has some of the positive effects on brain chemistry and mood mentioned above, all agree that Duchenne smiles provide *all* of these positive effects.

So when you smile in such a way that you engage both your lips and your eyes, you set off a complicated chain reaction that impacts your physiology and your emotions in myriad positive ways.

If you want to take advantage of the positive mood-enhancing effects of a Duchenne smile, a useful means of doing so is recalling an incident that made you smile genuinely. Simply recalling that incident can trigger the muscles to create a Duchenne smile and make it easier to tune in to the immediate benefits of such smiling.

But the most interesting thing about smiling is that it not only affects you in a direct physiological and psychological manner, it also impacts those around you.

Smile though your heart is aching,
Smile even though it's breaking ...
You'll see the sun come shining through.

— Charlie Chaplin, entertainer

Emotional Contagion

The phenomenon of "emotional contagion" has been researched a lot over the last several years. That research has proved what we all instinctively knew – emotions are infectious. One person can infect another with his or her moods and emotions.

Emotional contagion was originally a survival mechanism. We developed it to enable us to read each other's state of mind and emotions. In more primitive times, tuning in to someone else's panic at the presence of a threat often meant the difference between life and death. In modern times, that programming can still be seen in those around us. Look what happens when a plane suddenly hits a particularly heavy patch of turbulence. Many of the faces in the cabin instinctively scan the faces around them to determine if there's a threat. The canny ones scan the faces of the experienced cabin crew. If their faces look panicked, then the panic begins to spread and amplify, often wordlessly.

We have evolved the ability to unconsciously read a huge amount of information from the facial expressions of those around us.

One recent study (by Joyce E. Bono and Remus Ilies) concluded:

> Results of our studies clearly indicated that leaders' emotional expressions play an important role in the formation of followers' perceptions of leader effectiveness, attraction to leaders and follower mood. Our results also suggest that charismatic leadership is linked to organizational success, at least in part, because charismatic leaders enable their followers to experience positive emotions. More importantly our results indicate that the behavior of leaders and managers can make a difference in the happiness and well-being of the followers by influencing their emotional lives.

Emotions are contagious.

Our emotions affect our facial expressions, and others read our facial expressions. In fact, really effective readers of facial expressions can sometimes seem able to read the minds of those around them.

The process by which emotions are transmitted from one person to another is called "mimicking." Humans tend to mimic the facial expressions of those around them. If you doubt it, think of the last time someone yawned in your company (did you almost yawn just thinking about it?). We are natural mimics.

One of the many studies on the topic of mimicking was undertaken by Sweden's Lund University. It confirmed that we instinctively mimic the facial expressions and bodily state of those around us. In doing so, our brains translate these mimicked facial expressions and bodily states so that we experience the same emotions as the person we are mimicking. In this manner, emotions and mood are communicated from one person to another via facial gestures.

> When one person feels good and smiles, he or she sets off a chain reaction. That person is mimicked by those around him or her and they, in turn, enjoy a boost to their mood. This makes them smile more and so the cycle continues.

Of course, it can work in reverse too. We also mimic negative facial expressions. This "chameleon effect" (as researchers Tanya Chartrand and John Bargh call it) goes a long way to explain the so-called "mob mentality," in which negative emotions like anger are mimicked and re-mimicked, rapidly amplifying and exponentially raising the emotional intensity of a situation in seconds. It also explains why funny movies seem so much funnier in the company of others and horror movies seem altogether more frightening in a crowd. It's all about the physiologically and psychologically infectious nature of moods and emotions.

This is the mechanism great method actors use to evoke a genuinely emotional response in their audiences. They analyze the way their characters would feel and recreate those emotions in their own minds. In doing so, their faces adopt exactly the associated facial expressions and thereby effectively transmit their desired moods and emotions to their viewing audiences.

This emotional contagion has great implications for those whose stage is the workplace, where charisma can have such a dramatic impact on employee engagement and productivity.

So What Does This Mean for Your Quest to Be More Charismatic?

Harnessing the charismatic impact of smiling is absolutely core to raising your leadership charisma. The effects of smiling read like a definition of charisma itself. After all, if you can consistently change others people's moods for the better – if you can make them feel more positive, energetic, and self-confident, then it's fair to say that you've gone a long way toward creating a charismatic persona.

> If charisma is your aim, then our advice really couldn't be more straightforward – smiling genuinely must become a standard part of your normal daily behavior. You need to become an Olympic-class smiler – a purveyor of positivity, positive feelings, and mood enhancement.

Practice by smiling at service personnel – parking-lot attendants, retail employees, waiters – everyone you encounter. Don't expect anyone else to get the ball rolling by smiling at you, and don't deny someone the benefit of your smile just because that person looks grouchy or humorless. That may be the very time your smile can do the most good. Don't budget your smiles – they cost you nothing.

The more you smile at others, the more they'll smile at you; the more they smile at you, the better you'll feel; the better you feel, the more you'll smile at others …

It is a genuine no-downside deal. By raising your mood and your confidence you will raise the mood and confidence of everyone you encounter – and raise your charismatic impact dramatically, even with total strangers.

You'll notice that sharing your smile is like lighting someone else's candle from yours. It doesn't diminish the light from your candle in any way whatsoever; it creates much more light for everyone. You can raise the mood of an entire group with your smile.

Start now, and persist. This is a public service – one that will reward you in bucketfuls. A classic example of "paying it forward."

We Can Think of Just Four Reasons Why You Might Not Do This

Smiles are rarer in most everyday workplaces than they should be. Now that you're aware of the potential impact of this potent nonverbal cue, we can think of just four reasons not to harness this in the service of driving a more charismatic impact on people.

1. **You're self-conscious about your smile**

   Lots of people are. Get in front of a mirror and practice until you get a smile that a trusted adviser, your spouse or a friend, tells you looks confident and inviting. Then practice recreating it. Make a point of remembering the next real-life incident that makes you smile, and thereafter recall that experience any time you need that smile again. This is a good way to recreate a genuine Duchenne smile.

2. **You're too reserved**

   That's OK, but the only way to work through it is practice. The first few times you try, especially with strangers, it will feel strange and uncomfortable. Persist and it will become second nature. You'll find the attitudes of those around you changing right away.

3. **Your teeth are not great and you don't like showing them**

   Get them sorted out. This is an investment in building your charisma and it will be repaid many times over by the increase in your self-confidence and the impact you have on others.

4. **You couldn't be bothered**

   Your choice – but forget any thoughts of charisma.

Smiling, Charisma, and the Workplace

Every workplace has its own emotional microclimate – and the day-to-day weather is set by those in charge.

Even when things are tough, charismatic leaders create an emotional climate that lifts the moods of their people, providing them with the energy, optimism and motivation to keep pushing for the results they need.

For this reason your choice as to whether or not you employ your facial expressions, and other nonverbal behaviors, in the service of a positive workplace is gone the moment you take on a leadership role. You no longer have any real choice. You must learn to make smiling a standard part of the way you behave from day to day – especially when things are tough and smiling is the last thing you feel like doing. It's your job to be as charismatic as you can. Charisma gets results.

Charismatic leaders create extraordinary loyalty in their people because, consciously or unconsciously, their people know that they can always depend on them for the transfusion of positivity and energy they need to keep pushing ahead. If the boss is anxious and worried then the team will be too. If he's upbeat and optimistic that mood is transmitted. Displays of worry and anxiety are a luxury the charismatic leader chooses to forgo.

At the start of every day, make a point of greeting your people with a personal smile, greeting, and word of encouragement. Raise the mood in the workplace one smile at a time – and look out for a more positive type of "mob mentality."

When you're being introduced to someone new, hold off on sharing your smile until you've been given his or her name. Then, as you shake that person's hand, look into his or her eyes and deliver your best Duchenne smile. The impact of holding your smile for this moment is enormous. It looks like that person's name and the experience of meeting him or her is the most positive experience you have had all day long. You've won a friend.

It's not enough to smile occasionally, or when you're feeling good. It must be consistent. You must continually build a workplace where all feel privileged to be there, working alongside someone who has such a positive impact on their mood and their lives – alongside a charismatic leader.

Don't Underestimate the Power of a Smile

There is no sustainable charisma without smiling. If you don't harness this critical nonverbal behavior, you'll work very much harder to develop the charismatic impact you wish to make on others.

Once you have your smile turned to full beams, you can enhance its impact even further by engaging your eyes in the nonverbal communication process, as you'll read in Chapter 9.

The Eyes
Have It

9

So, YOU HAVE mastered a strong, confident posture that clearly communicates to people, even at a distance, that you have many of the traits of a charismatic person – self-confidence, energy, and positivity.

You have learned how to intensify your charismatic impression as those people approach a little closer, by engaging the power of a full-on Duchenne smile. This not only intensifies your confident and energetic impact, but it also transmits some of your positive mood, energy, and confidence into the minds of those you smile at. You've made the people you encounter feel better – and your physical charisma has been immediately intensified.

Now, as those people get closer still, you'll want to really cement that charismatic impression by deploying another extremely powerful nonverbal tool – eye contact.

Why Eye Contact Is Critical to Charisma

A key component of sustainable charisma is trust – and a key component in communicating trustworthiness is eye contact.

Eye contact cranks up the emotional energy in any encounter and can forge an immediate and positive connection between you and those you interact with.

Failing to make eye contact with others sends a variety of messages, depending on the relationship between the two people in question. None of these messages is positive. At best, a lack of eye contact can send the message that you are shy and lacking in self-confidence – an impression that's offensive to no one but you. At its worst, a lack of eye contact can suggest arrogance or superiority, but is most often (mis)interpreted as dishonesty, untrustworthiness, evasion, nervousness, lack of interest, or shiftiness.

Look at expressions we use daily that refer to eye contact: "Look me in the eye and tell me that" or "She just couldn't look me in the eye." Lack of eye contact creates an extremely uncharismatic impression.

On the flipside, those who can maintain eye contact make a longer-lasting and more positive impression of self-confidence, honesty, and trustworthiness. As with smiling, there is a positive feedback relationship between eye contact and confidence. Making more eye contact makes you feel more confident; more confidence makes it easier to make eye contact, and so on.

How to Make Positive Eye Contact

Start the first time you meet someone. When you're being introduced to someone new, look him or her in the eyes as you're given his or her name. As you grasp his or her hand in a firm handshake, hold that eye contact and open up your best Duchenne smile, smiling with your lips and your eyes. The charismatic impact of giving the person both barrels (your smile and eye contact) is enormous.

Then, as you continue to speak with the person, maintain comfortable eye contact. Don't stare fixedly; be sure to break away from his or her eyes every three to five seconds. A good strategy to avoid a staring look is to choose a few different spots to focus on around the other person's general facial area. For example, looking at just one eye helps reduce the appearance of staring. After three to five seconds of looking at someone's left eye, for example, move your gaze smoothly to his or her right shoulder for three to five seconds, then back to his or her right eye smoothly for another three to five seconds, then the left shoulder and so on.

It sounds peculiar, but the overall impression is one of good eye contact without any uncomfortable staring effect.

Just one point: make your transitions smoothly. Don't look like you're scanning from left to right like the carriage in an old fashioned typewriter, or bobbing your head up and down like one of those novelty nodding animals you see on the back windows of automobiles. The transitions must be smooth and natural.

You should aim to be in eye contact somewhere between 70 and 80 percent of the time. Any less seems less than interested and any more can be too intense. This punctuation of your eye contact with breaks every few seconds avoids an excessively probing or aggressive impression and prevents you from deteriorating into an uncomfortable stare. You're not in a "who blinks first" contest.

Groups

When you're engaged with multiple people in a conversation, beware of the "puppy dog" approach of switching from one face to another too quickly. Take three to five seconds of comfortable eye contact with one, then gently and smoothly switch to another. Unless you're making a point, be sure to share that eye contact equally among the group.

As you move around a room you'll find yourself establishing eye contact with others as you pass, and in some situations you won't want to engage with them. That doesn't mean you should deny them eye contact. You can still reach out to them and make a charismatic impression by acknowledging their existence through the use of your eyes.

Simply engage their eyes for a few seconds, nod and smile. This recognizes the other person. The combination of eye contact with a full smile has a very positive and charisma-enhancing impact, without necessarily signaling a desire to converse further.

Learn From Those Around You – and From the Pros

Watch those around you – look at their eye-contact behaviors. What works? What doesn't? What makes a powerful impression on you; what makes you uncomfortable?

Learn from those who use eye contact well, and then apply those lessons in practical situations as often as you can.

To really master eye contact, watch how the pros do it. Carefully watch your favorite TV interviewer and become a student of the way he or she uses eye contact. Then emulate it. How does he or she make a strong point, express agreement or disagreement, create rapport, express surprise and so on? Great interviewers have great eye contact. Learn from them.

Up Close and Personal

Develop your eye-contact skills and combine them with a good posture and the conscious use of your Duchenne smile and you have the holy trinity of nonverbal tools that charismatic leaders use to enthrall people. Apply all three and you'll see your charismatic impact improve immediately.

Having mastered the long-range nonverbal effect of a strong posture, the medium-range impact of your Duchenne smile, and the short-range effect of good eye contact, you are now ready to harness a powerful nonverbal medium you can use when you're up close and personal with others. Chapter 10 tells you how to harness the power of touch for charismatic impact.

The
Charismatic
Impact
of Touch

10

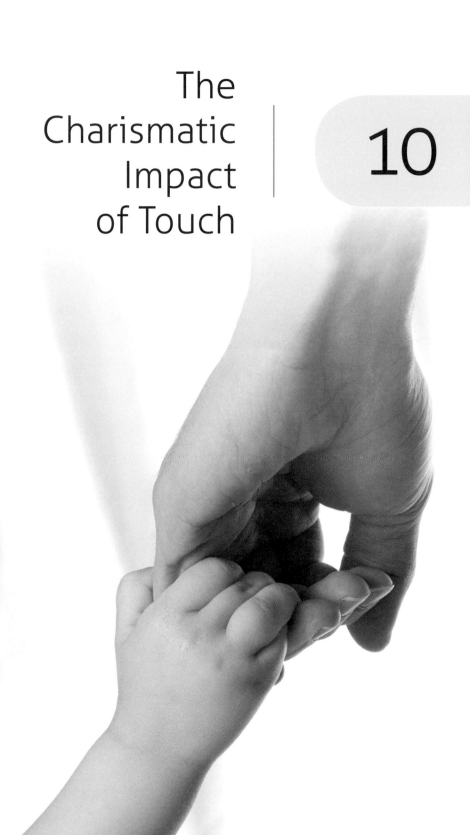

As the largest organ in your body, representing about one fifth of your total body weight, and one absolutely covered with nerve endings, your skin is one of the most important interfaces you have with the world around you and those in it.

The moment you were born you experienced the comforting and healing power of touch. A mother's touch can ease a child's pain, calm his or her anxiety and soothe him or her to sleep. And the impact touch has on you and everyone else around you doesn't diminish as you age.

Touch is so much a part of our behavior as humans, it is so primal in its impact on us, that you won't find it surprising that it is always associated with those perceived widely as charismatic. In your quest for charisma, touching appropriately is something you'll need to master.

The Power of Touch

Matthew Hertenstein, a psychologist at DePauw University in Indiana, found that blindfolded candidates touched by complete strangers could distinguish eight distinct emotions ranging from love to gratitude or disgust. "We used to think that touch only served to intensify communicated emotions," he said, but his research shows that touch is a "much more differentiated signaling system than we had imagined."

You can communicate an enormous amount through the simple act of touching another person – agreement, sympathy, encouragement, support, gratitude and more.

You can reassure, support, praise, console, or even correct using the swiftest of touches. Touching can calm the angry or anxious, raise the spirits of the depressed, reassure and comfort the grieving. Consider comforting someone in grief. Which is more effective: some comforting words or putting an arm around his or her shoulder/taking his or her hands?

But good touching is also beneficial to those doing the touching. Just like smiling, touching or hugging triggers the release of dopamine and serotonin, the two "feel-good" hormones mentioned in Chapter 8 in association with smiling. It also triggers a reduction in cortisol, the hormone that promotes the feeling of stress.

> For both the person touching and the person being touched, touching reduces stress, raises immunity, lowers blood pressure, and raises self-confidence. Not a bad résumé for something that's so easy to do.

Touch and Bonding

Touch is very closely wrapped up with trust, and trust promotes bonding.

The first time your mother touched you, your baby's brain triggered the release of oxytocin, the hormone that promotes trust and accelerates bonding. This is what intensifies the bond between baby and child. But oxytocin doesn't go away as you grow and mature. Even now, someone touching you triggers the release of this hormone and promotes a greater feeling of trust for the person initiating the touch. Charismatic people develop great bonds with people, so the importance of touch to charisma is clear.

This has extraordinary effects on everyday interactions. A study by the Cornell University School of Hotel Administration revealed that wait staff who touched their customers more got significantly higher tips.

Touch, and the resulting release of oxytocin, can even immediately create a stronger bond between two strangers. In a controlled experiment in a restaurant, waiters were instructed to make a meal recommendation to patrons (there was a control where some waiters made no such suggestion). For half of the recommendations, the waiter was instructed to touch the patron slightly on the forearm while making the suggestion. For the other half, they made the suggestion verbally only. The suggestions accompanied by the brief touch were much more successful than the suggestions alone.

Touch is a powerful bonding agent. With your goal of creating a charismatic bond between yourself and others, touching appropriately and often is something you must master – especially if you intend to harness that charisma in the service of getting greater engagement and cooperation from your people as a leader.

Touching and Gender

According to body-language guru Allan Pease, women are four times more likely to touch when communicating.

Given the bonding effects of touch and the implications for contributing to your perceived charisma, this is great news for women. However, it is also good news for those men who learn how to harness touch appropriately as an element of their charismatic behavior. The fact that it is not so commonplace for men means that those who get it right will indeed stand out from those around them.

Where and When to Touch

Where you can touch another person varies greatly from culture to culture and you'd be well advised to acquaint yourself with local culture and traditions should you find yourself away from home. Don't assume that what is acceptable for you at home will be acceptable elsewhere.

For example, in Latin America, the *abrazo* or hug is commonplace. This full-body hug is so normal in that culture that you'll appear very standoffish and cold if you don't give and take hugs freely. For some people in North America and the UK, this is just a little too "full on" to be acceptable; for others it's a way of life. Across Europe the level of touching that is acceptable varies widely, with France, Spain, Italy, Greece, and other Mediterranean countries having a much more touch-oriented culture than countries like the UK and Netherlands. The Arab world also tends to have appropriate gender-to-gender touch integrated into its culture.

For this reason you should focus on perfecting the way you touch others using the level that is maximally acceptable across the majority of cultures you'll encounter.

Pretty much everywhere in North America and Europe, it is generally acceptable to touch someone on the shoulder, elbow, arm, or hand, as long as the touch does not last too long. Two to three seconds is more than long enough to have the desired effect without having any unwanted impact.

Be careful not to use touch to reinforce negative points – it can come across as aggressive. Focus on using it to support positive points.

Even a brief tap on the forearm as a sign of reassurance or agreement can be extremely powerful and reassuring. The traditional brief pat on the back can also be very encouraging, as long as the accompanying language ensures that it does not seem in any way patronizing. A tap on the hand or lower arm while making a positive point can cement that point. These brief and non-threatening gestures are very frequently a standard part of the communication styles of those perceived as charismatic.

Touch can very often communicate in situations where words simply will not do the job.

Worldwide there are a very wide variety of greeting rituals, ranging from hugging, cheek-kissing, "air-kissing," rubbing noses, "high fives" and many more. Perhaps the most universal of all touch-based greetings is the handshake. It is practiced and accepted in pretty much every culture to some extent or other – especially in business situations.

Touch Can Dramatically Affect Business Culture

Every January the 1,000 + business partners of Profiles International come from all over the world for their annual conference. The entire event is an education in the power of touch – and has to be the biggest annual "hugathon" in the United States.

Thanks to the culture of hugging established by the two founders very early in the organization's history, most of these people routinely greet one another with hearty hugs. The late Jim Sirbasku always insisted that everyone needed "at least eight hugs a day." That, he insisted, was essential just to maintain a healthy sense of well-being.

The result? All attendees talk of the bond that they have both with one another and with the organization at large. "There is no event quite like a Profiles conference. Not only are people entirely open to sharing all of the ideas that work for them in their businesses, but you get a real sense that all consider themselves to be part of something altogether bigger. It's almost a family-type atmosphere," commented one attendee. Another said, "I never miss a Profiles conference. Quite apart from the mass of useful business information it provides, the event is always energizing and optimistic – and I always come away feeling much more connected to the hundreds of people I have befriended in the business over the years."

The bottom line is that Profiles has an extremely strong and cohesive culture using touch as an integral part of the relationship-building process. Profiles enjoys an extraordinarily high retention rate for business partners. "We don't have a problem with employee or partner turnover at all," commented one senior executive.

Handshakes

The experts speculate that the handshake evolved from a primitive need to prove trustworthiness by offering an empty hand to show the absence of a weapon.

Offering anyone the opportunity to touch any part of your body is in itself an act of trust – so the handshake is very much an act of mutual faith.

Handshakes have all the benefits associated with other forms of touch discussed above, but it would be reasonable to assume that the handshake is such a commonplace act that its impact is likely to be more dampened than that of other gestures. Even so, according to a study by the Incomm Center for Trade Show Research, you are twice as likely to be remembered by someone you shake hands with than by someone you don't.

As the primary touch opportunity you get with just about everyone you meet, it is important that you get the handshake right if you are to enhance your charismatic impact on others.

How to Shake Hands

There are dozens of body-language books that go into excruciating detail on the subject of the handshake, and all of the power-play that can be associated with this simple act.

As someone interested in making a charismatic impression, you want your handshake to send a positive message of interest and friendliness. You want it to say that you acknowledge the other person as having great worth and value. So forget the power games of offering your hand palm down to give you the "upper hand," don't determine to crush the other party's fingers to show how forceful and strong you are, and avoid the politician's two-handed shake that seems so false except with someone so close that you would be just as comfortable hugging him or her. Keep it simple.

Here's a basic handshaking guide.

- Before you initiate a handshake, ensure that you are face to face with the other person to convey an open and honest impression.

You should stand with your arms by your sides, with the palms outward – a comforting stance for the person about to meet you. Avoid standing side on to someone you're greeting. A side angle communicates a less trustworthy image.

- A first handshake normally follows on the heels of a verbal introduction by yourself or another person. As the verbal introduction is made, extend your hand, thumbs up, fingers together and straight.

- Make sure your hand is pushed gently into the other person's hand so that the web between your forefinger and thumb makes contact with the web between the other person's forefinger and thumb. Otherwise you get one of those weak finger-shakes that is uncomfortable for both parties. When the two webs "dock" with one another, grasp the other's hand gently.

- Give two to three gentle pumps from your elbow, and then release. Don't pump them wildly up and down – a few inches of movement is sufficient.

- As you shake, engage your Duchenne smile (Chapter 8), smiling both with your lips and eyes – and make firm, friendly eye contact. The previously discussed physiological impact of your smile, along with the physiological impact of your touch, will be remembered positively.

- Release as the introduction ends. Holding on longer can seem like a play for power or an intimate act and is uncomfortable for many people.

A few other points on handshakes:

- Don't use the macho bone-crushing handshake that so many male businesspeople favor – it conveys an entirely wrong impression if you're trying to promote your charisma. If another engages in bone-crushing behavior, don't bother to compete.

- If you're prone to sweaty hands, try to wipe them discreetly before you grasp the other person's hand.
- If you shake hands with someone whose hands are sweaty, resist the urge to wipe your hands afterward until you can do so discreetly without embarrassing the other person.
- Beware the double-handed shake unless you know the other person very well. The clasped handshake, where the other person's hand is cupped in both of yours, is like a hug. As a general rule, use it only where you'd be equally comfortable hugging the other person.

Harness the Power of Touch

All of the research on this topic suggests that charismatic people use touch as an integral part of their communication. Simple touches to the forearm of another will reinforce your agreement when you're of the same opinion and will help maintain open communications when you're not. A hand on the shoulder or pat on the back will reassure. Even momentary touches like the "high five" have an enormous impact in helping you bond more closely to others.

As with anything else, one of the most effective ways to perfect this behavior is to observe those who do it well. Look at those you deal with on a daily basis. How do they touch you? What makes you react positively? What do you find uncomfortable? Watch effective politicians, successful businesspeople, charismatic celebrities, and public figures and learn from how they use touch. What works for one person in your culture will work for all, when harnessed and used to help you reach out and establish a genuine positive relationship with others.

If you touch someone appropriately, you will come across as more open, friendlier, warmer, and more caring. You'll also be perceived as altogether more genuine and trustworthy – two of the precursors to being perceived as charismatic.

Your Nonverbal Lexicon Nears Completion

With posture, smiling, eye contact, and touch under control, you have a firm understanding of how to harness your body to maximum effect in making a charismatic impact – even when you're doing little and saying nothing. The last dimension of physical charisma that is directly associated with your body – gesture – is covered in Chapter 11.

Charismatic
Gestures

11

B Y NOW IT'S clear that everything you do is absorbed by those you deal with just as much as everything you say.

We've already looked at the communication powerhouses of posture, smiling, eye contact, and touch. Body and hand gestures are no less important.

All of the research on gestures says the same thing – gestures communicate nonverbal messages that are every bit as strong as the verbal messages we intend to transmit.

A recent study by Spencer Kelly, Associate Professor of Psychology, Colgate University, showed that people were much quicker to understand any verbal message when the message was supported by appropriate gestures. When the gestures either were missing or didn't match, the message was harder to understand.

What's more, research reveals that when your words and gestures do not match and you send conflicting messages, the person you communicate with will believe the gestures and other body language and ignore your verbal message. Your gestures speak much more loudly than your words.

So, for the charismatic wannabe, mastering and harnessing gestures is absolutely critical.

Some Gesture Vocabulary

Gestures reveal your inner attitude – something you'd sometimes prefer to keep private. Warm, friendly gestures include leaning toward people, facing them squarely, touching them, smiling, and using positive facial expressions.

Lack of eye contact, absence of a smile, hidden palms, hands on hips, drumming, fidgeting, playing with clothes or jewelry, picking nails, and so on are perceived as cold or nervous gestures. Watch your expression in unguarded moments.

There are some core gestures, however, that are almost like gesture "phrases" that can be combined to tremendous positive or negative effect. By understanding those, you'll choose to use them to your advantage.

- Palms

  Your palms convey an enormous amount of information when engaged in a gesture. In general, if your palms are down or hidden from view you are seen as closed and authoritative. The gesture says, "I'm in charge," or, "This issue is not up for discussion." Palms facing up are seen as open and say the opposite: "Trust me," "I'm friendly," "You're my peer," "Let's talk," or, "I'm open to discussion."

- Leaning in

  When you like someone or are interested in what he or she has to say, you unconsciously lean in. Everyone does. Similarly, when you do not like someone you unconsciously lean away from him or her. This is so ingrained in us that we are all unconsciously capable of reading this critical signal very effectively. So any time you want to indicate interest or a positive attitude toward an individual or audience, lean in slightly.

  Be particularly wary of leaning away from someone in an unguarded moment. Unless you've made a conscious decision to send a message of dislike, distrust, or indifference then this is too powerful a message to get wrong. Become aware of whether you're leaning in or out. If in doubt, don't lean out!

- Nodding

  This is another simple but very telling basic gestural phrase. Nodding indicates interest and encourages other people to continue doing or saying what they're doing. Not nodding sends a neutral or even uninterested impression. Once again, unless you're trying to signal lack of interest, use frequent nods accompanied by encouraging sounds to signal that you are positively interested to hear more of what they have to say. Be careful, however, to use single, well-spaced nods. Double or triple nods in quick succession are the same as saying, "Speed up!" or "Get to the point!" Eye contact is great reinforcement here.

- **Relative position and openness**
  Standing square to someone, as long as you're not too close to him or her given your relationship (see "Personal Space" below), is a friendly and open statement – especially when the view of your solar plexus is unimpeded by your hands or other objects like desks, lecterns, and PCs. Standing at an angle signals an unconscious desire to get away, to find someone more interesting to talk to, or to protect yourself.

Create a "Safe Position"

Many people tend to be reasonably confident that their gestures are pretty positive once they are in the full flow of a conversation or presentation. It's in the quiet lapses in between that they start to feel uncomfortable and become unstuck. You need to establish a habit of returning to a good, positive "safe position" between gestures, from which to launch your next stream of body language.

The easiest and most effective such position, and one you should perfect, is very straightforward – but it takes a little practice to make it a habit. First, correct your posture using the approach outlined in Chapter 7. Then consciously relax your shoulders to get rid of any unnatural stiffness in your appearance. Let your hands hang loosely by your sides with the palms open and reasonably visible.

Part your feet approximately to shoulder width, put one foot slightly forward to balance yourself, then lean in toward whomever you want to pay attention to.

Now you're in a relatively relaxed and positive position from which you can easily launch any of the other required gestures as you speak. Practice returning to this safe position when you are between gestures or simply standing there, waiting to be introduced on stage, for example, or listening to a question during a presentation.

Personal Space

You have a "no-fly" zone around you – and the less intimate others are with you, the further out that "no-fly" zone extends for them.

Edward T. Hall established the concept of personal space. He also established that one of the greatest of all nonverbal communication sins is to invade another's personal space. Humans have an extremely strong physiological reaction to their personal space being invaded. It is suspected that this reaction is driven by a very old and primitive part of the brain, the amygdala. The general reaction is "dehumanization." Think of the way people react on a crowded train or elevator where they are forced into uncomfortably close physical proximity that intrudes on their personal space. They switch off totally from those around them, pretending they do not exist, ignoring their very humanity and tuning their existence out completely. Be wary of completely grounding communication with another by the simple act of moving too close to him or her.

If you move forward to make a point and the other person moves back shortly afterward, you have invaded his or her personal space – albeit without meaning to. Allow the other person to settle at the distance that makes him or her most comfortable.

It is critical to realize that the concept of personal space is highly elastic, from culture to culture and place to place. The personal-space needs of someone living in a densely populated city will be quite different from those of someone living in the Australian outback.

Hall established the personal-space parameters for North America as:

- Intimate: 18 inches and less.
- Personal: 18 inches to 4 feet.
- Social: 4–12 feet.
- Public: 12 feet to the edge of visibility.

This can be safely applied to most English-speaking countries and to many northern European countries. Southern Europeans, however, often tend to have smaller personal-space parameters and, to their northern cousins, can seem to stand too close by far. Latin Americans have a smaller sense of personal space and may see an American as standoffish or cold if he or she adopts the customary American personal-space distances. In Asia most of the literature suggests that it is a non-issue and that people expect much less in terms of available space.

When in environments that are unfamiliar to you, observe the way other people interact and the personal space they observe, and adapt your spacing to match. If in doubt, allow your conversational partner to lead the personal-space dance.

The critical message is: know the acceptable personal space in each culture, taking your relationships with the people you're talking to into account, and then ensure that you do not encroach on anyone's territory.

Seven Charisma-Enhancing Gestures

Here are seven really powerful gestures that combine the gesture vocabulary above to provide you with an extremely effective set of gestures that have a universally positive and powerful effect. You should learn them, understand where they should be applied, and immediately begin to integrate them into your communications with others – whether on a one-to-one, one-to-many (presentation) or one-to-camera basis.

- "I have nothing to hide"
Stand upright with good, straight posture and relax your shoulders so that you're not too stiff in appearance. Position your feet at about shoulder width, one slightly farther forward than the other (to steady yourself), and lean in slightly. Hold your elbows at about 90 degrees and turn your hands to your conversation partner or audience, palms up, fingers slightly splayed, showing them your fully open palms. Make sure they have an unimpeded view of your solar plexus.

   An alternative version that gives the same effect and can give you variety, especially when presenting to a large audience where you want to make yourself look bigger on a stage, is to spread your arms out from the shoulders, again with your hands and fingers up, with your palms facing forward fully.

- "From the heart"/"I mean this sincerely"
Bend your elbows so that the palms of your two hands are facing your chest; bring your slightly splayed fingertips in so that they almost touch your sternum, with fingertips pointed toward your chest.

- Authoritative but not aggressive
Use this in any situation where you'd love to be able to use the generally aggressive and negative gesture of pointing your forefinger. Instead of pointing with your forefinger, bring your forefinger and thumb together and relax your other fingers alongside these two.

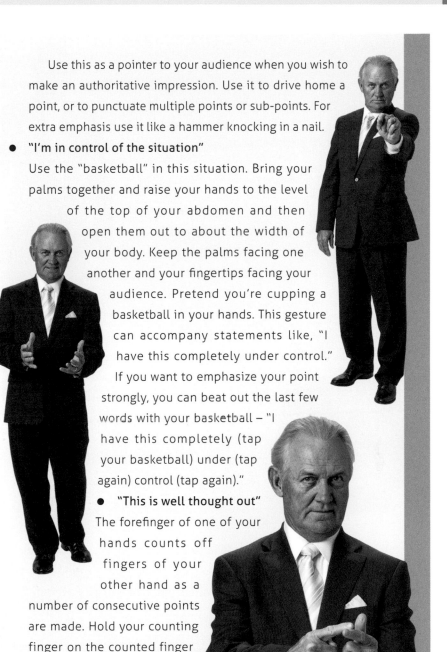

Use this as a pointer to your audience when you wish to make an authoritative impression. Use it to drive home a point, or to punctuate multiple points or sub-points. For extra emphasis use it like a hammer knocking in a nail.

- **"I'm in control of the situation"**

Use the "basketball" in this situation. Bring your palms together and raise your hands to the level of the top of your abdomen and then open them out to about the width of your body. Keep the palms facing one another and your fingertips facing your audience. Pretend you're cupping a basketball in your hands. This gesture can accompany statements like, "I have this completely under control."

If you want to emphasize your point strongly, you can beat out the last few words with your basketball – "I have this completely (tap your basketball) under (tap again) control (tap again)."

- **"This is well thought out"**

The forefinger of one of your hands counts off fingers of your other hand as a number of consecutive points are made. Hold your counting finger on the counted finger until your point is fully made ("Step 1 ... step 2 ...").

- **"That's that"**

  This is just like a karate chop. The chop signifies a definitive point, one that is not in doubt or up for discussion. It signals, "I'm finished," "That's that," or, "End of discussion."

- **"Steepling" of the fingers**

  Steepling of the fingers conveys a high confidence in whatever you are saying, and a lot of research has shown that it has a large impact on the credibility of your message. Steepling is most often seen used in a sitting position, with the steeple at about chest level and the steepled fingertips facing the ceiling. However, it is equally effective when used in a standing position, as in the picture on the left." Don't overuse it – and be careful not to let a steeple degenerate into interlaced fingers. This looks more like a wringing of your hands – and conveys a low level of confidence in your message.

These seven gestures are so powerful that you should make a particular point of practicing them until using them effectively becomes second nature. Use a full-length mirror, and, if you can, run them past others to get their input on how you can make them more effective.

Negative Gestures to Avoid at All Costs

Here are some classic negative gestures that, having read this chapter, you will notice in others around you. Most of them are so obvious that no one allows themselves to use these gestures consciously. That's the danger of these "tells" –

most of them are used completely unconsciously. You need to become conscious of your every gesture, and, if you spot one of these, you need to work on consciously eliminating it. Replace it with an alternative, positive gesture from the list above.

- **Hands near your face**
  Rubbing your eye or touching your nose, ears, hand, or neck as you speak. Touching your nose is the typical "I'm lying" gesture you'll see detectives in TV cop shows use to identify guilty suspects (despite the fact that lying is notoriously difficult to recognize definitively from gestures or body language alone).

- **Hands over mouth**
  This says, "I'm not sure of what I'm saying" or "I'm trying to deceive."

- **Arms crossed**
  This is one of those postures that everyone has read about in relation to body language. Some cultures read this as defensive and closed, even though some people use it simply as a perfectly comfortable resting position. In general it is a defensive posture only when it occurs suddenly in reaction to some external stimulus – something someone has said or done. Arms suddenly folded and locked tightly are clearly defensive. For the simple reason that it could be misunderstood by amateur body-language readers as defensive, closed or negative, it's best simply to avoid using this gesture.

- **Hands over your genitals**
  Highly defensive and nervous. Never a positive message.

- **Objects in front of your body**
  PCs, desks, lecterns – anything that creates a distinct separation between you and others again indicates defensiveness. Don't hide your solar plexus.

- Hands in pockets ...
  Something to hide.
  ... and rattling your change
  Nervous and ill at ease.
- **Clenched fists**
  Obviously anger, right? Many people unconsciously clench their hands and signal anger or displeasure they have otherwise managed to conceal. Be aware of it and don't let it slip in unconsciously.
- **Drumming fingers or tapping toes**
  Impatience: "Aren't you finished yet?" Another behavior that many people exhibit unconsciously – and that signifies irritation very clearly.
- **Pointed forefinger**
  This is threatening, aggressive, and overly authoritarian. No one likes to be pointed at in this manner. Adapt the alternative, more positive version outlined above under "Authoritative but not aggressive."
- **Checking your fly, playing with your watch, shooting your cuffs, straightening your tie, or white knuckles on the lectern prior to speeches and presentations**
  Nervous and unsure of yourself. Shoot your cuffs, straighten your tie and wind your watch before you take the stage. Then use the "safe position" described above.
- **Hands on hips**
  This can be used to signal power and readiness but is frequently read as aggressive. Be careful.
- **Arms behind your back**
  This strongly sends a "stay clear" message – "I don't want to make contact with you or talk with you." If that's the message you want to send, that's fine. If not, be cautious.

Mirroring

When talking with someone, make it a habit to take a few minutes to observe how he or she gestures while speaking. What does he or she use to make positive or negative points, emphasize things, or express positivity or negativity? Once you have observed some of that person's more common gestures and are confident that you understand the context in which he or she uses them, then you can build rapport by reflecting some of those gestures.

Do not mimic the person parrot-fashion or copy him or her faithfully as if you were following a choreographed routine. Simply recognize his or her gestures and feed back your version of them when making similar points. The impact is quite dramatic – it establishes the sense that "this person really understands me" or "we really are in tune on this issue." Only use the more positive of the person's gestures (and, if they impress you as being particularly effective and communicative, continue to use them afterward as part of your gesture repertoire).

Inventory Your Gestures

Start to observe your own gestures and the gestures of those around you. If any negative gestures have slipped into your gesture vocabulary, focus on replacing them with more positive alternatives.

Observe those around you who have a charismatic demeanor. What gestures do them employ? When you see something that communicates effectively and suggests the charismatic impact you're aiming for, then assimilate it and make it your own.

Research by Maxwell Maltz (originator of Psycho-Cybernetics) suggested that it takes 21 days of practice to make anything a habit – so don't expect this to become second nature without some conscious focus and practice.

The more you tune your gestures to the positive so that they emphasize the already-positive message you're sending through the medium of your posture, smiles, and eye contact, the more your entire physical message will align with the behaviors discussed in Step 4 to dramatically increase the charismatic impact you have on those around you.

Step 4

Create a Charismatic Leader's Persona

Step 4
Create a charismatic leader's persona

Step 3
Fine tune your physical charisma

Step 2
Build a foundation for your charisma

Step 1
Make a decision to become a charismatic leader

You've Come a Long Way!

I N WORKING THROUGH Steps 1 to 3 of the Leadership Charisma Model you made a commitment to becoming a much more charismatic leader. If you have begun to apply the lessons from those first three steps, you will already have noticed a distinctly more self-confident version of yourself emerging and will be seeing people react to you in an altogether different manner.

You'll recall that in Chapter 1 we defined leadership charisma in a very specific way that emphasized the results you wish to achieve from those who work for you.

Definition: Leadership Charisma

Charismatic leaders create and maintain a work environment where people are emotionally and intellectually committed to the organization's goals. They build an energetic and positive attitude in others and inspire them to do their very best. In doing so they create a common sense of purpose in which people are more inclined to invest extra energy and even some of their own time in their work.

In Appendix I we outline the research undertaken with more than 40,000 leaders and their hundreds of thousands of direct reports. That research identified a very specific set of behaviors that will trigger a charismatic response in those who work for you.

This final step will take you step by step through making those charismatic leader behaviors a part of your normal behavior as you go about the day-to-day business of leading your team.

Assessing Your Current Leadership Charisma

Some wise businessperson said, "You can't manage what you can't measure" (W. Edwards Deming is usually credited). Absolutely correct.

If you can't measure how charismatic you are right now, how can you decide precisely what to do to raise your leadership charisma in the most efficient manner possible? If you simply follow each of the four steps laid out in this book, you will definitely see a dramatic increase in your charismatic appeal as a leader. However, it is almost certain that you already have some of these behaviors well tuned and contributing to your current level of charisma – so why spend more time on them? That's time and energy you could invest more profitably in developing behaviors that don't already serve your charisma so well. Wouldn't it make more sense to focus your energies on improving those areas that need additional focus – those behaviors that, with a little additional fine tuning, will immediately increase your charismatic appeal? That's where an assessment is invaluable.

From the outset we were keen to create a set of assessments that would allow leaders to measure the extent to which they were currently viewed as charismatic and identify any areas needing development.

We created two measures of leadership charisma designed to provide leaders like you with a snapshot of how charismatic they are currently seen to be, and guidance on how to raise that charisma.

1. Leadership Charisma Index (LCI).
2. Leadership Charisma Quotient (LCQ).

1. **Leadership Charisma Index (LCI)**

   Several times throughout this book we have said that charisma, like beauty, is in the eye of the beholder. Your LCI provides you with an overview of how charismatic you are currently seen to be by those people who work for you right now – your direct reports.

   This obviously requires input by your direct reports. To avoid biasing the results your people are not asked to provide input on your charisma as such. Instead, they are simply to provide input on your everyday behavior as a leader using the 70-item Checkpoint system outlined in Appendix I. We later assess that input to produce a report for you that provides you with your LCI score.

   That report not only presents you with your current LCI score, but also provides you with more guidance on those areas you should focus on developing in order to begin to raise your leadership charisma day by day.

2. **Leadership Charisma Quotient (LCQ)**

   At time of writing we had data on leadership-charisma ratings, and on ratings of the 70 Checkpoint leadership behaviors, for more than 40,000 leaders worldwide. That number grows every day as hundreds more complete the Checkpoint daily around the world.

   Using that data we were able to create an average Leadership Charisma Index for all 40,000 of those leaders. By comparing your Leadership Charisma Index to that global average we can give you a very accurate assessment of how your current level of leadership charisma compares with an enormous audience of charismatic leaders worldwide. We call that comparison your Leadership Charisma Quotient (LCQ) and we calculate it as follows:

Leadership Charisma Quotient

$$\frac{\text{Your direct-reports Leadership Charisma Index}}{\text{Typical global Leadership Charisma Index}} \times 100$$

If your LCQ is greater than 100 then that is an indication that your direct reports see you as being more charismatic than is typical in our global sample. If your score is less than 100 it tells you that your direct reports see you as being less charismatic than is typical in our global sample.

Your LCI tells you how you're doing with your current direct reports. Your LCQ goes a step further and gives you an idea of how your leadership-charisma rating ranks on a global basis.

How Charismatic Are You Now?

Your LCI and LCQ are wonderful reality checks on your current leadership charisma in that they provide you with a direct comparison of your view of your own leadership charisma versus that of the people who deal with you from day to day – and give you a great starting point for your leadership-charisma-development efforts.

Before you dive into this final step of working on developing your charismatic leader's persona, wouldn't it make a lot of sense to know just how charismatic you are at the moment? Wouldn't you like to know which charismatic behaviors you already naturally exhibit and which ones you're going to need to work on developing?

The Final Step in Becoming a Charismatic Leader

The results of our research were exactly what we had hoped for. They provided a clear connection between specific learnable leadership behaviors and the perception of leadership charisma, and they gave us the final critical input we needed to create the final step in our Leadership Charisma Model – which will allow anyone to take a step-by-step approach to raising his or her charisma as a leader.

The following chapters will take you through the process of assimilating the behaviors that are critical to being seen by your direct reports as a charismatic leader.

Step 4 is the final step in the Leadership Charisma Model. It includes seven vital chapters:

- Chapter 12: Charismatic Communication
- Chapter 13: Inspire with Your Vision
- Chapter 14: Be Contagiously Energetic and Enthusiastic
- Chapter 15: Be a Beacon of Positivity
- Chapter 16: Be *the* Expert in Your Field
- Chapter 17: The Charismatic Power of Belief in People
- Chapter 18: Recognize the Greatness in Others

Charisma and Communication

In our research (Appendix I) communication came out top of the list of behaviors having an impact on the perception of a leader as charismatic. This, of course, implies that the most important skill set for an aspiring charismatic leader to continually develop and hone is his or her ability to communicate. In and of themselves, great communication skills do not necessarily make a leader charismatic. It takes emphasis on the other five areas too.

However, it is obvious that leaders who do not have above-average communication abilities put themselves at a serious disadvantage charismatically. Even if they do everything else right, who would know? Communication is critical to bringing your charismatic qualities and behaviors to the attention of those around you.

This is reflected in the very first chapter of this critical final step, with its large emphasis on communication as a means of driving charisma.

Charismatic Communication

12

C OMMUNICATION SKILLS ARE a decisive factor in developing your persona as a charismatic leader.

In the introduction to Step 4 you saw that, in our research, communication was cited by the hundreds of thousands of employees rating their leaders as being a critical element in driving their perception of charisma.

It makes obvious sense. If charisma is, as we discussed in Chapter 1, very much in the eye of the beholder, then it's obvious that superior communicators will communicate superior charisma.

It's clear: no communication, no charisma. Highly polished communication skills are critical to the development and maintenance of a productive charismatic leader's persona.

This didn't surprise us in the slightest. We were aware (from research by Schnake *et al.*) that most managers spend 50–90 percent of their days communicating. All of the formal research we undertook, combined with straightforward observation of the extent to which modern business leaders who were described as charismatic tended also to be described as great communicators, meant that we went into our research acutely aware of how important communication skills are to the development of a charismatic leadership style.

What we hadn't anticipated was quite how important communication skills are in determining a leader's charisma. In our study communication alone accounted for more than any other single factor in high charisma ratings for leaders. Communication behaviors contributed almost 40 percent to respondents' ratings of those leaders they identified as being notably more charismatic than the norm.

Communicating for Charismatic Impact

Communication is an enormous topic – one on which hundreds, if not thousands, of books have been written. Similarly, there are hundreds of courses on all aspects of communication. If you're serious about becoming a more charismatic leader, about getting your people so engaged that they achieve the sort of above-average results genuinely charismatic leaders achieve, then you're going to need to become serious about continually polishing your communication skills.

You'll need to devote time to reading, training, and coaching that will, on an ongoing basis, raise your ability to communicate. This is a lifetime endeavor. There will always be room to be a better communicator, just as there's always scope to become more charismatic than you already are.

Communication is probably the most essential part of my job.

— Marc Benioff,
founder, Salesforce.com

Charismatic Communication – Not Solely about Presentation Skills

When businesspeople think of charismatic communication they almost inevitably think of great presentations – of a presenter lighting up the room with his or her presence. Being able to deliver great presentations undoubtedly raises your charisma significantly, especially where you are guiding a team through challenging times or in pursuit of a challenging vision or goal. Good presentation ability is a great platform for continually reinforcing your charisma with your target audience. There is nothing so motivating as a rousing "get-up-and-go" talk from a talented presenter.

So the leader who seeks to be more charismatic must continually work on the improvement of his or her presentation skills – which is why the second part of this chapter is devoted to charismatic presentation skills. But presentation skills are not enough on their own. You may have had the experience of working with a wonderful presenter who, offstage in everyday situations, had little or no charismatic appeal at all. Or you may have had the experience of working with someone who was a poor presenter but still managed to garner genuine charismatic appeal in everyday situations.

The reality is that a lot of the type of charisma we attribute to what we defined as charismatic leaders (those who engage their people so intensely as to get superior productivity from them) is driven more in everyday communication situations than it is in grand speeches. Charisma is really about communicating one on one or in small groups with those working directly for you.

In the first part of this chapter we address everyday one-on-one charismatic communication. We suggest you focus on this initially. This will have an immediate impact on your charismatic appeal to your people.

In the second part of this chapter, we look at the subject of presentation charisma.

The combination of these two aspects of communication have a genuinely synergistic impact on charismatic appeal. Either one will increase it significantly, but add the two together and the impact will far exceed your expectations. In this instance one plus one makes an awful lot more than two!

Continually improve your ability in both of these areas and you'll see your charismatic appeal, and the results you achieve from your people, soar.

Charismatic Communication I: The Everyday

In one way this is a brief look at everyday communications for charismatic impact. But, in the sense that it covers the *minimum* that you need to be doing to be a charismatic leader, implementing the advice in this chapter alone – such that these key communication behaviors become an entirely natural part of your day-to-day way of communicating with those around you – could become the work of a few months. You don't need coaching or courses to make these ideas work. If you have made the decision to be charismatic then you can make the decision to start implementing these ideas immediately. Make that decision, commit to improving your communication, and you'll make these critical communication behaviors part of your normal *modus operandi*. It's up to you.

Here are seven key aspects of one-on-one communication you should work on perfecting day by day before you start thinking about anything more elaborate. We guarantee you this – implement any of these ideas that are not already part of how you communicate from day to day and *you will* see your charismatic impact on others rise. It's unavoidable.

The Charismatic Equation
The extent to which you are perceived as being charismatic is directly proportional to the extent to which people either feel or fare better after each interaction with you.

Seven Secrets of Charismatic Communication

We all love the idea of secrets – which is why the title of "seven secrets" appealed to us for this section. In reality none of the following is a secret. But we see them so seldom applied consistently by leaders charged with getting superior results from their people that they might as well be. Charismatic leaders are still very much in the minority – because of a simple failure to assimilate these straightforward behaviors.

Now that they are all listed in one place, there are no excuses for leaders not to dramatically raise their charismatic impact on their people in a very short time.

The Seven Secrets of Charismatic Communication

1. Keep it upbeat.
2. For heaven's sake, listen!
3. Communicate one on one.
4. Solicit ideas, opinions, and suggestions from others.
5. Communicate in a straightforward manner, even when dealing with sensitive subjects.
6. Create a comfortable climate for raising concerns.
7. Display common courtesy.

1. Keep it upbeat

Even if you hadn't already seen it in action, common sense would tell you that leaders who maintain a positive communication environment will always outperform those who don't.

Remember the Charismatic Equation? Your communication must be so positive that it lifts your people in a real way each time they interact with you and with the environment in which you put them to work. To raise your charisma as a leader it's essential you create a positive communication environment.

● Reject negative expression

Anything that can be said negatively can be said positively to much greater effect. Even criticism can be delivered in a manner that is more positively than negatively charged. Rigorously police your own everyday language and communications to root out any negative messaging. Consciously drop all negative vocabulary from your everyday use. Refuse to engage in negative expression yourself – and reject it utterly from any member of your team. Make it clear: you run a positive ship.

- **Watch your nonverbal communication**

  Just because you cut out negative language doesn't mean that you don't communicate negative messages – especially to those with whom you don't have the best possible relationship. Understand the messages on physical charisma from Step 3, and ensure that your facial expressions, body language, and general nonverbal behavior express a positive, open, and non-critical demeanor. Non-critical does not mean undemanding. You can demand the highest standards, and harshly critique the most heinous mistakes, without ever resorting to toxically negative expression.

- **Find the good news – and promote it**

  There is always something good to communicate. Why then do so many environments degenerate into a perpetual focus on discussion of what's *not* right? Work on improving things that didn't work out – but don't become obsessed by the negative. If you focus on the negative you'll simply program everyone to get you more of it – and you won't be surprised when they do! Recognize that good news travels much more slowly and much less widely than bad news. So when something good happens, when there's a positive message to convey, communicate it again and again. Don't be concerned about over-communicating good news – it's unlikely to happen (especially as most people have an insatiable appetite for the positive).

- **Be humorous**

  Humor is highly charismatic. Everyone likes to laugh, and those who give us opportunities to look at the lighter side of life are always in demand. Used properly, humor can break down barriers between people with completely different perspectives, or from entirely different cultural backgrounds. In everyday situations humor helps to create a generally more positive environment.

Some people are natural comedians, with a quip or a joke to suit every occasion. If that's not you, don't worry. Just make a decision to be open to looking on the light side in every situation. There will be humorous people in your group. Foster an environment where they share their humor with the group at large. But make sure all keep it positive. Stamp out any negative humor, rude attacks on others or their ideas, and any sort of discriminatory behavior.

If you create an environment where people have fun while still achieving great results, they'll enjoy working with you and you will become more charismatic in their eyes.

2. For heaven's sake, listen!

You've heard and read it a thousand times – but unless you are a perfect listener, and few of those exist, then it bears repeating. Listening is one of the most critical communication tools.

It's very easy to spend time with good listeners. They make you feel important; they make you feel like what you have to say is the most important thing to them at that point in time. And that's why listening has such a charismatic impact. Make me feel important and valued and I'll find you charismatic – it really is that simple.

Two of the foremost political rivals in the United Kingdom in the nineteenth century were William Gladstone and Benjamin Disraeli. Both of them were extraordinarily successful, but they had vastly different approaches to people. A young lady who dined with them separately later said:

> [W]hen I left the dining room after sitting next to Mr. Gladstone, I thought he was the cleverest man in England. But after sitting next to Mr. Disraeli, I thought I was the cleverest woman in England.

BusinessWeek columnist Carmine Gallo said of former US President Bill Clinton:

> Clinton looked me in the eyes and seemed to have a genuine interest in what I was saying. His gaze never left me. He made me feel like the most important person in the room at the time, and Microsoft founder Bill Gates was standing right next to us!

That's charismatic communication at its very best. And with a little practice it's easy!

The Disraelis and the Clintons of this world do not become such great listeners by accident. It's all about conscious practice of this critical charismatic skill. Unless you put time and effort into perfecting your listening skills you will not reach these heights.

INTUIT INC.

[I]n conversation he listens unlike any other leader I have ever seen. Listening, he seems to forget himself. He seems composed of pure curiosity. He's like a man who always expects that the next thing that someone – anyone – tells him might be the most surprising and enlightening thing he has ever heard. He listens without blinking. He learns.

— Michael Hopkins, magazine editor,
on Scott Cook, founder, Intuit

- **Be in the moment**
  When someone is speaking with you make it a point to give them 100

percent of your attention. Start by making eye contact. Apart from all of the charismatic impact of eye contact that you read about in Chapter 9, doing so reminds you where your focus should be. If you feel yourself drift away to other concerns, then stop yourself. Assure yourself that everything else can wait – you'll get to it later. But if something else is just too distracting, don't try to fake it – you'll fail. Consider asking the other person if you can come back to the topic on another occasion. Go and clear the other issue, then return to the conversation and devote yourself 100 percent.

- **Listen carefully without interrupting**

  The majority of people spend most of their conversation time listening in their own minds to what it is they plan to say next. Do so and you'll inevitably end up interrupting. Your enthusiasm for your contribution will overcome your interest in what the other person is saying. The moment you do that you send a clear message that what you have to say is more important than what the other person has to say – as uncharismatic a message as you can get. Every time you find yourself wanting to interrupt, resist the temptation. Instead, do the polar opposite. Implement the next suggestion – summarize what has been said to you.

GETTY IMAGES

[T]ry not to speak until the other person has said the last syllable of what they are saying. Waiting for one second after your employee or colleague has said their last syllable will create a more communicative and trusting culture ... In that one second the human brain is able to have an enormous number of thoughts so you get a different dialog because there's been a larger universe considered.

— George Zimmer, founder, Men's Wearhouse

- **Summarize input and check for understanding**
  One of the most effective ways of ensuring that you listen actively is to practice feeding back your understanding of what you've heard to the other person. "So what you're saying is ..." or, "If I understand what you're saying, then ..." Do it regularly during the conversation. Not only does it assure your conversation partner that you understand what he or she is saying, but it also gives you an active way of keeping yourself focused on him or her. Other-person focus of this kind is a classically charismatic trait.

- **Listen to all points of view with an open mind**
  Develop a reputation as someone who is genuinely prepared to take all perspectives into account before making a decision. Decide to become genuinely open enough to consider that others may have a point of view that is as valid as, and perhaps even more valid than, yours. Resist the habit of rejecting others' points of view just because they run contrary to your own. Instead, give everyone a fair hearing and honestly assess the value of their contributions before making a decision on how you feel about them.

3. **Communicate one on one**
   The best communication time you'll ever spend with people is one-on-one time. Make a particular point of scheduling regular one-on-one sessions with each of your people. Despite the obvious wisdom of this basic suggestion, this is not common practice. But this is one of the most critical secrets of the success of all charismatic leaders. They genuinely know their team. In later chapters we'll talk about what you should do when you do meet with each of your people in this manner. But at a very minimum:

- **Congratulate them**
  Everyone does something worthy of note on a daily basis. Make it your business to be aware of something notable they have achieved since you last spoke, and, before anything else, congratulate them on it and thank them for their contribution.

> Sometimes the fiercest thing we can say to someone is, "I want to tell you exactly what I appreciate about you."
>
> — Susan Scott, author

In *Fierce Leadership: A Bold Alternative to the Worst "Best" Practices of Business Today*, Susan Scott suggests you tell your team members exactly what it is you appreciate about them – without a "but" or a "however" within ten miles of your conversation. Appreciate them and they'll appreciate you. This directly leverages the Charismatic Equation, driving each person's self-esteem through the roof – with your charisma trailing only slightly behind it.

Always open on a similarly positive note.

- **Remind them of their value**

  Make sure that you are clear about your people's different roles in achieving your vision – how they can contribute and why their contribution is so essential. Then remind them frequently. Don't assume that they know. Make it a point to explain why their input is so critical and how their contribution will be key in getting your team where it wants to go.

- **Review progress against goals**

  We all need to feel that our contribution is valuable – and we need to know where we stand. Make it a point to ensure that you review your team members' goals with them individually at least monthly, or more often if you can.

  That exercise will keep you informed and connected – but it will also motivate them. In Chapter 17 you'll learn how to use this time to set the self-expectations of each of your people so that they strive to reach levels of performance they never thought themselves capable of. Reviews like this are the perfect opportunity to do just that.

- **Make current job-related information available**

  The ancient thinking that "information is power" – and that those who hoard it maintain their power – is dead. Charismatic leaders tend to get the maximum from their people by openly sharing with them as much information as they can. This enables team members to feel positive and motivated about the environment in which they work. Openness breeds charisma.

- **Take them into your confidence**
Some things you'll share in group meetings; some things you will not. There is nothing as flattering as the feeling that someone else trusts you enough to take you into his or her confidence. Don't "spill all of your candy in the lobby" in group meetings. Always hold back something that you can share later in one-on-one meetings with members of the team on a "just me and you" basis.

Extending trust creates trust. Trust is a keystone of charisma.

- **Talk to them about themselves**
Showing a positive genuine interest in each of your people's personal lives and personal goals is not just a great way to get an insight into how to motivate them more effectively, it also creates a much more personal relationship.

  Those observing charisma in another have the sense that person really understands and cares about them and their personal situations and concerns. That is one of the principal features of the charismatic relationship.

- **Ask for advice**
In each meeting with a member of your team, have some topic on which you specifically need to ask that person's advice. And when you ask, then listen to the advice you get. Get him or her to open up and share advice, expertise, and ideas with you. Build a two-way bond that will foster your charismatic appeal.

Leadership is communicating to people their worth and potential so clearly that they come to see it themselves.

— Stephen Covey, author

4. **Solicit ideas, opinions and suggestions from others**

   Most leaders make the mistake of assuming that they understand what's going on in the minds of those working for them. Don't assume.

Make it a point to solicit feedback from all of your people on a regular basis – in one-on-one encounters and in group meetings. Ask, "How would you go about this?" or "Is there another way we could achieve ...?"

   Regularly put each of your people in a situation where they have to contribute, and they'll come up with input you never expected. When they do so you make them feel bright and valuable – and instantly raise your own leadership charisma. At the same time, you get valuable input that will make everyone's life easier.

   • **Involve everyone**

   Some people have no problem providing feedback in your everyday meetings and in other public forums – but some will shy away from this. Make it a point to seek input from those who hold back in group meetings. Most people who hold back in this manner do so because of lack of confidence in what they have to say. Build their confidence by calling on their input every so often in group sessions. Ask them, "What's your take on this, David?" or "How would you do this, Marie?"

   If you still find it difficult to get them to contribute in such forums, then get time with them one on one and solicit their ideas. Making another feel valuable is one of the most charismatic acts possible – and a critical way of doing so is simply to ask for their input and suggestions. You'll build their own confidence in the value of their insights – again, raising your own charismatic impact. In every conversation make it a point to ensure that you have taken ideas, opinions, and suggestions from *every* party to the conversation before you make any decision or determination.

- **Follow through**

  The first time you take feedback, nod sagely and interestedly at the suggestions – and then proceed to do nothing whatsoever to follow it up – is the last time you'll get valuable feedback. The feedback loop remains open, and a charismatic impact is achieved only when you close the loop by being seen to take some action. When you act on feedback you applaud the contributor and encourage more feedback.

  Even if, having considered someone's contributions, you must later come back and explain why that feedback did not result in the action he or she would have liked, this is vastly preferable to simply ignoring input you do not like.

5. **Communicate in a straightforward manner – even when dealing with sensitive subjects**

   Life is not a bowl of cherries, and sometimes you will have to deliver the nastiest of news to the nicest of people. How you do this will largely determine the extent to which people will trust you – which is critical. No trust, no charisma.

   The principles below focus mainly on delivering bad news to a group. But you should have the same concerns, and do the same preparation, when you must deliver bad news to an individual.

- **Clarify the facts**

  If you must deliver bad news, be certain that you are in full command of the facts before you consider broaching the topic with anyone. Get all of your facts straight. If the topic is complex, then clarify it in your own mind by writing it all down. Write it down in such a way that even someone who had nothing to do with your environment would understand what you're trying to say. You may never share this with anyone, but it will clear your own mind and ensure that you have thought all aspects of the issue through.

Think of any questions that might arise, and prepare answers. Again, writing down your Q&A will be very helpful in clearing your own mind.

- **Be clear**
Deliver your message so that the facts are made totally clear and leave no room for speculation. Don't pad your comments with unnecessary commentary or "weasel words." Say your piece clearly and without decoration. Deliver the facts without hesitation. Watch to make sure that everyone is understanding your critical points – and restate key facts if you have any doubt. Make it easy to understand.

- **Do it now**
Bad news has a way of leaking, and the longer you put off announcing it, the more risk you run of a leak undermining your ability to manage the situation effectively. Rumors and speculation can frequently be more damaging than the bad news you must deliver. Do it now.

- **Let people ask questions and express concerns**
Schedule enough time to make sure everyone affected by the news gets an opportunity to ask questions and express concerns. There is nothing more damaging than a rushed announcement of bad news followed by a hasty adjournment before people have an opportunity to digest what it means for them. It'll make you look weak and underhand – pretty much the opposite of charismatic. Don't run away. Stand and support those affected by the bad news, however uncomfortable it may be for you.

Then map the way forward. When people are affected by bad news, that's when they most need leadership. Once they have had an opportunity to absorb the implications of your news, show them what happens next. Talk about the next actions you'll take. This refocuses people away from the bad news and onto how you plan to get yourselves back on track in meeting your shared vision.

- **Don't lie**

  All you need is one lie to be uncovered and your entire charismatic persona comes crashing down in a pile of broken trust. If you don't know then say so – and, if appropriate, commit to finding out what you can to share later. If you know but are not at liberty to discuss it, then say so. Always tell the complete truth – and tell it as early as you possibly can.

- **Don't hide behind language**

  This is almost worse than lying. Use straightforward, everyday language – don't use language and word choice to distract from the facts.

The years 2008 and 2009 saw a large number of layoffs in organizations worldwide. In many of those situations those announcing the layoffs believed themselves clever in using language to hide their true message. Here are a few examples we found on the web:

- "implement a skills-mix adjustment."
- "initiate a career alternative enhancement program" (US car manufacturer who laid off 5,000).
- "assign candidates to a mobility pool."
- "eliminate redundancies in the human-resources area."
- "a volume-related production-schedule adjustment" (reduction of 8,000 jobs).

It seems that everyone can see the completely untrustworthy nature of such communication – except those who engage in it. Don't be one of them.

Spit bad news out in plain English. Anything else erodes trust, and when trust is gone charisma is impossible.

6. **Create a comfortable climate for raising concerns**

   Unless your people can express opinions contrary to yours, or to those of other more assertive or senior members of the group, without fear of any negative consequences, then the most assertive and loudest voices will always have their say and valuable input from others will be lost. Make a point of having no "sacred cows." Anyone should be able to express his or her opinion or raise concerns without worrying that there may be consequences. Create a safe environment for open and frank exchanges.

● **Provide opportunities to vent**

   Make sure that you provide regular opportunities for your people to vent their frustration or concerns in either one-on-one or group sessions. Make it clear that you value such input and feedback and that you expect it from everyone. Be prepared to accept that you will sometimes hear things you wish you hadn't. Be prepared to accept criticism and contrary opinions and to weigh them for their genuine value. Encourage straight talking, and practice losing all ability to take offense when someone disagrees with you or offers a contrary point of view. Disagree if you must do so – but do so agreeably.

7. **Display common courtesy**

● **"Sorry" seems to be the hardest word**

   There is nothing more powerful (because sadly, it is so unusual) than someone in authority owning up when they are in the wrong. If you offend someone, speak inappropriately angrily with them, argue incorrectly against the merits of their case, or offend anyone in any way, then make a point of apologizing.

   Be bigger than the majority. Don't hide behind weak self-justifications or behind your authority. Make amends. If the offense was committed in public, then the apology should be in public. If it happens in private, then it can be in private.

When you apologize, do not couch your message in "weasel words." It's better to give no apology than to offer the always-insulting non-apologetic apology. You know the sort – it typically begins with words like, "If I offended you in any way then I'm certainly prepared to apologize ..." or "If you felt that I was in any way wrong in the way I treated you then I'd like to say sorry ..." Humility and genuine contrition on the part of someone who has the authority to get away without apologizing conveys a respect for others and a level of honesty and truth that is so rare that it makes you stand out. Such honesty is extremely charismatic.

- **Be responsive**

  Everyone is too busy to respond instantly to every e-mail they receive. If you receive a message about something important to one of your people, but so low on your priority list that you won't be able to respond quickly, simply send a one-line thank you, explaining that you received the note and when you'll be able to respond. This sends a clear message – your time and your concerns are just as important as mine.

- **Please and thank you**

  In Chapter 17 we will explore this in greater detail but it merits some mention here too. Both of these so-called common courtesies are no longer as common as they should be.

Want to make someone feel valued? Ask them, "Could you help me out with something please?", "Would you be able to do me a favor?" or "Please help me figure out something out."

Use "please" liberally – even if what you're asking for forms a key part of their job responsibilities. Then, when they perform the service, be sure to say thank you. The more people present when you express your gratitude to someone, the better for that person's self-esteem. Remember the Charismatic Equation. If another person comes away from you with his or her self-esteem in better shape than when he or she first met you, then you are charismatic to that person.

- **Hold your tongue**

  In the pressure of a heated argument or disagreement any of us can get so caught up in the emotional whirlwind that we find ourselves saying something we normally wouldn't wish to – and the moment we say it we know it. The problem is that this particular bell, once it has been rung, cannot be unrung. You can take it back – but it's altogether better not to have said it in the first place.

  In a heated exchange, in writing or in person, disengage when you feel the emotion carrying you away. Take five. If it's a one-on-one situation, seek to create an opportunity for each party to go away and reconsider his or her position, with a view to trying to reach an accommodation acceptable to both parties later on.

  This is particularly true of disagreements that escalate over e-mail. E-mail is a wonderfully instantaneous communication medium, but sometimes it seems like its negatives outweigh its positives. E-mail communication tends to be open to miscommunication because of the instantaneous manner of its exchange. Too many people live to regret e-mails written in the grip of powerful emotions.

  Don't communicate in anger or frustration.

Before you press "send" and transmit a stinging e-mail response to a perceived offense, force yourself to stop and think. Dale Carnegie taught that you should write out all you would like to say, and then put it away in a drawer overnight. For e-mails you should do the same. Save your emotionally charged missile in your "drafts" folder until you have had a chance to cool down. Overnight is ideal. Things always look different the next day.

Focus on the Everyday

As a leader you will spend a good deal of your time on everyday one-on-one communications – so this is the logical place to start raising the communication skills that are such a key factor in creating and maintaining a charismatic leader's persona.

Apply these seven charismatic communication behaviors, assimilate them and make them a natural part of how you work on a daily basis, and you'll see your charismatic impact on your people rise dramatically.

Charismatic Communication II: Public Speaking, Success and Charisma

Clichéd research tell us that the majority of people fear death more than speaking in front of a group. Whether that's true or not, it is undoubtedly true that fear of public speaking is a real issue with a great many people, which probably explains the fact that those who can really deliver a persuasive or motivating speech are more frequently seen as charismatic and successful than others.

A study conducted by AT&T and Stanford University revealed that the top predictor of professional success and upward mobility is how much you enjoy and how good you are at public speaking. In that study the single best question to predict high earnings was, "Do you enjoy giving speeches?"

Being able to deliver a good talk to a group will get you further faster than pretty much any other skill you can learn and develop. The ability to do it better than the average puts you head and shoulders above those around you.

But good speaking is also an extraordinary contributor to the perception of leaders as being charismatic. Stop and think of the most charismatic people you know of. For English-speaking nations that list often includes names like Martin Luther King, Winston Churchill, and John F. Kennedy. Whatever else the people on your list share in common, you'll find, as we did with ours, that all of them share an above-average ability to speak to groups.

Public speaking is the shop window that allows the wider world to see the charismatic dimensions of people who, in one-on-one situations, excel in the sort of superior charismatic communication we covered earlier in this chapter.

The ability to speak well will allow you to expose your charismatic appeal to a much larger audience, and with much greater impact, than you could any other way.

There is a common assumption that accomplished speakers know more about their subjects than any of the rest of us. Whether that's true or not doesn't matter – this is the respect that the majority of people pay to good speakers. Speak well and you'll be thought of as an authority on your subject. Speak well and you'll also be accorded greater leadership skills by those who hear you. This all builds charisma.

> To build your charisma, build your speaking ability. A weak message from a good speaker will have much more impact than a strong message from a poor speaker, regardless of how much we'd like to think that the opposite might be true.

Clearly there is no more valuable skill set in the armory of the charismatic leader than the ability to address a group effectively.

> Hundreds of books have been written on public speaking, and we're not going to try to reproduce them here. If you've read all of the basics then you might be interested to read a few of our favorite books on the topic, which give a different perspective. Try reading *Win the Crowd: Unlock the Secrets of Influence, Charisma, and Showmanship* by Steve Cohen (a magician who talks about entrancing your audience!).

Creating a charismatic impression in a presentation or speech situation is not a lot different from doing so in a one-on-one situation. To imbue your speeches with a charismatic impact you must harness the same concepts and employ the same behaviors we looked at earlier in this chapter for improving one-on-one communications.

In more than 40 years observing Jim Sirbasku, our late co-author, an extraordinarily charismatic speaker, we have seen up close what makes for charismatic presentations and speeches. Combining those personal observations with the formal research discussed in Appendix I, and with the analysis of every recording we could find of those acknowledged as great charismatic speakers, we have identified nine simple things you can do to come across as a charismatic speaker.

Nine Ways to Become a Charismatic Speaker

1. Plan to be confident.
2. Look like a ten.
3. Exude energy and enthusiasm.
4. Warm the room with a smile.
5. Use your body effectively.
6. Use the "windows to the soul".
7. Use positive language.
8. Speak in images.
9. Use your voice as a charismatic instrument.

1. Plan to be confident

As you read in the introduction to Step 2, the beating heart of charisma is self-confidence. Your speeches will only have a charismatic appeal if you ooze self-confidence as you deliver them.

To be confident you must feel perfectly in control of the situation every time you speak – and that takes an investment of time and effort.

On an ongoing basis you must be working to develop your presentation and speaking abilities. Read as much as you can on the topic and take some sort of refresher training course, at least annually, to sharpen up your skills. Take as many opportunities as you can to get real-world experience as well. Continually hone your presentation skills.

With your basic presentation skills well under control, you'll automatically have a strong foundation for self-confidence in any public-speaking situation.

The only thing that could possibly undermine that confidence on the day is being ill prepared. If you know your topic inside out, have carefully prepared your content, and have rehearsed the talk several times before showtime, you'll know that (little or) nothing can go wrong. The confidence that comes from that knowledge will ensure that you'll walk tall and strong as you take the stage, confident of delivering an excellent speech.

Don't leave confidence to chance. Plan to be confident. Keep your presentation skills sharp, prepare carefully, and rehearse well and you'll always be confident on your feet.

2. **Look like a ten**

   We don't all look like Brad Pitt or Angelina Jolie – and it's not necessary to be handsome or gorgeous to have a charismatic impact on an audience. However, on your personal one-to-ten scale of how good you can look, make sure to give every audience ten every time. Show them the respect of looking your best.

   Look prosperous. Look like someone who has earned the right to their attention. Be impeccably turned out in every aspect of your clothing and personal grooming.

3. **Exude energy and enthusiasm**

   From the moment you walk on stage, you must exude energy and come across as enthusiastic about the opportunity to speak on your planned topic.

Don't drag your feet onto the stage. Stride out with a bounce in your step that shows how excited you are to be there.

When you feel passionately about one of your points, don't be afraid to show it. Use the sort of gestures you'll read about in the next point. Let your voice speed up and increase in volume. Scan the audience from face to face to ensure that they see your passion and your own belief in what you say.

Enthusiasm is highly contagious. If you're enthusiastic, your audience will be enthusiastic. Make the right impression on your audience and they will automatically make the judgment that anything that excites you and gets you enthusiastic must be worth hearing about.

Give them energy and enthusiasm and you'll be remembered for all of the right reasons – and they'll pay attention to what you have to say.

4. **Warm the room with a smile**

As you read in Chapter 8, smiling has an extraordinary impact on people. Turn on your best Duchenne smile and you'll have an immediate impact on the brain chemistry of anyone who comes into contact with that smile. The Duchenne smile not only lights your own brain up with the feel-good chemicals serotonin and dopamine (both of which raise your mood), it also has the same impact on those who observe your smile. As their brains are flooded with those same chemicals, they find themselves smiling even more genuinely. The resulting injection of even more of those chemicals into their brains reinforces this positive feedback loop and amplifies the feel-good factor for all. The simple use of the charismatic smile can dramatically change the emotional temperature in a room.

Your smile is a decisive factor in a setting the scene for a receptive audience and charismatic presentation. Use it well.

5. **Use your body effectively**

   Watch your body language. Your body language must communicate the same self-confidence, energy, and enthusiasm that you plan to deliver with your words. Use the guidelines in Chapter 7 to ensure that your posture makes the best possible impression. Walk tall, straight, and with deliberate purpose as you move around the stage. Pay attention to your posture throughout – a straight posture communicates confidence and ability.

   When talking, be sure to use the seven charisma-enhancing gestures outlined in Chapter 11 to emphasize your key points with the best possible body language. When you're standing on stage listening to someone else speak, or to an audience question, be sure to adopt the posture we described as the "safe position" to send the right body-language signals to those around you.

   Every member of your audience has developed an unconscious ability to read a huge amount of information from the body language of those around them. When your words and your body language are not consistent, people will *always* unconsciously trust your body language first.

   Be aware of what your body is saying right through your talk – and harness those charisma-inspiring gestures to send the messages you want to send.

   The eyes are the windows to the soul.

   — Ancient proverb

6. **Use the "windows to the soul"**

   Eye contact is a critical tool in creating a charismatic impression when you speak. When someone charismatic makes a presentation, everyone in the room feels that the person's comments are directed right at him or her. Eye contact plays a large part in creating this impression. If you can reach out and make every person in the audience feel that you are speaking directly to him or her during your presentation, the charismatic impact will be much greater.

CISCO SYSTEMS, INC.

Watching John Chambers deliver a speech is like taking a course in confident body language. He maintains eye contact more than 80% of the time and speaks directly to individual people in the audience, instead of looking randomly about over the heads of his listeners.

— Carmine Gallo, *BusinessWeek* columnist, on John Chambers, Chairman and CEO, Cisco Systems, Inc.

When addressing a large group, break the audience into three imaginary zones – center, left, and right. Make a point of scanning the entire room about every 30–45 seconds. Start with one of your imaginary zones and select someone to establish eye contact with. For about five seconds or so address your points directly to him or her. A large circle of people around that person will feel that you are addressing your points to them personally.

Then move your attention to the next zone and select someone new to address your attention to for another five seconds or so, making eye contact.

When you've done this with the last zone, work your way back across the audience in the opposite direction, doing the same thing. Each time you settle in a zone, select someone different to make eye contact with. Try to cover that zone from front to back over the course of your presentation so that by the end of your presentation you will have covered the entire room with a matrix of eye contact, and each person in the room will feel that you have addressed him or her personally at some point.

Charismatic impact is created one person at a time – and one of the best tools for achieving it when speaking to a larger group is eye contact.

7. Use positive language

People attribute charisma to those who have a certainty about them – those who seem to know what needs to be done and how they're going to do it and are confident of the outcome. Self-assurance, optimism, and confidence are very charismatic.

This has implications for your word choice in speeches and presentations. At all times your language must be self-assured and positive. You should display no uncertainty or doubt. There is no room for "hopefully," "if," "I hope," "if we're lucky," or other weak phrases.

Substitute these weak words with their more positive cousins. For "hopefully" substitute "certainly." For "if" use "when." For "I hope" use "I expect." Always use the most confident, optimistic language you can. If you sound uncertain then you will not convince your audience of your message.

Root out all negative language and replace it with its positive equivalent. Be positive and optimistic when you speak.

8. Speak in images

This is perhaps one of the most important pieces of advice for someone aspiring to be a charismatic speaker.

Think of the most powerfully charismatic and persuasive speech you ever heard. Got one? Now try to think of another. And another. Now stop for a moment. What do these great speeches have in common that made them so memorable for you? What made them so emotionally impactful, so charismatic, so persuasive?

You'll find that what such speeches share in common more than anything else is the use of rich emotional imagery to convey the speaker's key messages. Those speeches are memorable because they create in your mind a clear picture of the what the speaker wished to convey.

Whether it was Martin Luther King's "I've been to the mountaintop," or Winston Churchill's "We shall fight on the beaches, we shall fight on the landing grounds, we shall fight in the fields and in the streets," image-rich words light up a speech and make it instantly impactful and forever memorable.

Whether by instinct or conscious design, the most charismatic and most memorable orators from history have always harnessed the power of images to convey their messages in a much more powerful way.

In 2008 two researchers, Naidoo and Lord, scientifically proved that speakers employing images in speeches have measurably higher impact, not only on their listeners' emotional states but also, critically, on their perception of the speaker as being charismatic.

In their study, participants heard one of two versions of Franklin D. Roosevelt's famously moving 1933 inauguration speech. One of the versions of this speech retained the many vivid, emotional terms that characterized it and made it so impactful. The other version was identical in informational content, except the vivid, emotional terms were replaced with more abstract, conceptual words.

The version with the more vividly image-based language evoked much stronger positive emotional responses in listeners and dramatically raised later listener ratings of the speaker's charisma and leadership abilities by listeners. Naidoo and Lord proved that image-based communication was "more comprehensible, memorable, and emotionally involving."

Images speak straight to the listeners' subconscious and allow them to interpret what a speaker is saying in their own ways – and to connect it to their own experiences. This makes image-based speeches much more emotionally powerful.

Using Imagery in Your Speeches and Presentations

The great orators of history set what appears to be an impossibly high bar in terms of the often almost poetic or literary quality of their imagery. If you have a similar gift with language, then you have a headstart on those of us who do not. Use your lyrical turn of phrase to invest all of your talks with language that communicates greater emotion and deeper images. But it's not necessary to scale literary heights to make effective use of images that will render your speeches and presentations more memorable and charismatic.

There are tools that you can employ easily and effectively in order to invest your words with greater imagery and lift your talks and speeches way above the ordinary.

Five Image-Injection Tools

- Personal stories.
- Other's stories.
- Quotations.
- Metaphors.
- Similes.

- **Personal stories**

Everyone has a well of life experience to draw on in this regard – and the longer you have lived, the deeper that well is. Your life experiences can be among the most compelling illustrations you'll ever use – for the simple reason that they are so real to you. When you tell them, they will come across as very personal and impactful.

In his now-famous commencement speech to Stanford graduates in 2005, the charismatic founder of Apple Computers, Steve Jobs, based his entire speech on three stories from his life. First, he spoke of his early years when he was put up for adoption; then of how he felt when he was fired from his own company, Apple Computers; and finally he spoke of the effect that a brush with death, in the form of pancreatic cancer, had on him.

Because those stories were so obviously authentic, that audience was help rapt by his speech, and that talk is already being quoted as an all-time great business speech.

You too have such stories from your life – stories that made you who you are and taught you what you know. Don't imagine that they are of no interest to others; don't take them for granted. Your experiences can be among the most compelling assets you have in becoming a powerful charismatic speaker.

- **Others' stories**

You've often heard people close to you tell of their experiences and been moved by the lessons that can be learned from them. Your parents and loved ones have told you all sorts of stories about their lives and experiences – all of which can be wonderful instruments for getting a point across more effectively. Because they come from a different era, the life experiences of parents and grandparents can frequently be among the most compelling stories you can tell.

When you speak to groups from other cultures, always remember that the everyday stories and even myths that are familiar and ordinary to people sharing your background may be utterly fascinating to people from another culture.

Finally, there is nothing wrong with using the stories of great figures from history to make your points.

A good story is always the best way to make a strong point, regardless of the origin of the story itself. In general, try to use stories that are as close to your personal experience as possible, but don't hesitate to use *any* other stories that you feel will command your audience's attention and make your points more memorable.

- **Quotations**

  Isn't the Internet a wonderful thing? With it you have access to thousands of years of quotations from great leaders that can help you to hammer your point home better than you could ever do alone. When you use a quotation appropriately you effectively borrow the credibility of the person you quote. It's almost as if you have him or her up alongside you, helping you to make your point. And you can find a quotation to fit *every* situation simply by searching for something like "Quotations about <topic>."

  As Marlene Dietrich said, "I love quotations because it is a joy to find thoughts one might have beautifully expressed with much authority by someone recognized wiser than oneself." (We found that one by searching for "Quotations about quotations.")

  Quotations are a powerful way of both enriching your presentations and speeches with imagery and having a respected authority underscore the points you're making. Use them liberally.

I spend a lot of time creating metaphors to explain what we do. For example, early on we explained what we did with the metaphor "Salesforce.com is like Amazon meets Siebel Systems" [or] "the eBay of enterprise software."

— Marc Benioff, founder, Salesforce.com

- **Metaphors**

  Wikipedia defines a metaphor as: "an analogy between two objects or ideas ... For example: 'Her eyes were glistening jewels.'"

  Look at this simple example. Doesn't the "glistening jewels" metaphor tell you altogether more than any other set of everyday adjectives could have? The use of such imagery lights up the audience's imagination on a subconscious level and makes ideas and concepts altogether more memorable.

Michael Dell, the charismatic founder of Dell Computers, used a simple but extremely effective metaphor in a speech he made in 2003. He told graduates of the University of Texas in Austin to find their own way in life – "As you start your journey the first thing you should do is throw away your store-bought map and begin to draw your own."

There's no way you could make this simple message clearer or more memorable through the use of more conventional non-image-based language.

Make it a habit to write down useful metaphors any time you hear them. You never know when they will be of use.

There are dozens of reference books that will give you access, by topic, to metaphors for just about any message you want to convey. One excellent example is *I Never Metaphor I Didn't Like: A Comprehensive Compilation of History's Greatest Analogies, Metaphors, and Similes* by Mardy Grothe. There are lots more – check them out.

- **Similes**

   A simile compares two disparate things, generally using "like" or "as" to link them together and make the point more memorable. Similes are a fabulous mechanism for making a speech much more image rich and memorable – and there are thousands of similes on every topic imaginable.

   Our late co-author, Jim Sirbasku, was a great lover of similes. He often spoke of how our "sales took off like a homesick angel," of how good salespeople jumped on opportunities "like a rooster on a June bug," or how someone who looked a little grumpy had "a face like a bulldog chewing a wasp."

You can sprinkle similes right throughout your talk to inject a little color and, because similes are frequently humorous, you also give your audience a few laughs – which is a good idea when appropriate. Humor, as we have seen, is extremely charismatic.

As with the metaphors, make a point of writing down good similes you happen across – but you don't have to rely on those you've picked up. Once again, there are lots of simile dictionaries. *The Book of Similes* by Robert Baldwin and Ruth Paris provides an A–Z list of hundreds of great similes, all arranged by topic. There are lots more collections like this, and you'll even find some interesting lists sprinkled around the Internet. (Strangely, at the time of writing, we couldn't find a single online simile or metaphor dictionary. Could this be an opportunity for someone enterprising?)

Building Imagery into Your Speeches, Step by Step

When you have fleshed out your speech or presentation and you are absolutely clear on the key points you wish to get across, you can look at injecting some imagery into your talk to make those key points more memorable. Take this simple five-step approach to making your content more image rich, emotional, and memorable.

1. For each of your key points, brainstorm to see if any of your personal stories, or those you know of from others, might help to make your point more effectively. Look for stories that closely parallel the point you're trying to make.

2. If you cannot think of an appropriate story, search your metaphor and simile dictionaries to see if you can come up with anything that will help you drive your point home strongly and make it more memorable. Search the Internet to locate suitable quotations quickly.

3. When you inject your story, metaphor, simile, or quotation into your talk be sure that you have provided enough information in the build-up to it to make the point of your image crystal clear. Make sure the connection between your imagery and your point is perfectly obvious.

4. When you have illustrated your main points with suitably strong image-rich supports, look through your talk again to see if there is anywhere you could inject other metaphors or similes. Use them to punctuate your talk all the way through, keeping an element of imagery throughout. Be careful, however, not to overdo it. Don't string long lines of metaphors and similes together. Use these mechanisms like you use salt on your food – enough to make it interesting and tasty, but not so much that it dominates the meal or leaves too strong a taste in your mouth.

5. Try out your stories, metaphors, and similes on lots of colleagues, friends, and family *before* you use them in a public situation. Make sure they work well in making your point. Also, when you deliver your talk for the first time, watch your audience as you deliver each image. Did they get it? If not, elaborate.

You can raise the charismatic impact of any speech or talk you give in the future by simply investing a little time and energy in injecting a little more image-based communication. With so many average speakers delivering average material, you can distinguish yourself comprehensively by applying these simple guidelines to create image-rich talks and raise the charismatic impact of your presentations and speeches dramatically.

9. **Use your voice as a charismatic instrument**

Your voice is an endlessly versatile instrument. With the smallest changes in tone, volume, and inflection you can express the full range of emotions from depression to joy, from enthusiasm to apathy, from pessimism to optimism. Inject variations in tempo, volume, tone, etc. to make what you are saying interesting and to underline and emphasize key points with the emotional content only your voice can add.

- Always start your talk with a strong voice on high volume (take a deep breath into your diaphragm before you speak to eliminate any initial squeakiness).
- When making a critical point, slow down. Don't be afraid to slow down to a very slow and deliberate one-word-at-a-time pace for really critical points.
- Use the dramatic pause. Two to three seconds is like an eternity in a presentation. The sudden silence will jolt to full consciousness those whose concentration has drifted and grab their attention again. Use the pause when you have said something key and you want it to sink in. Silence makes people take note; it makes them replay in their minds what you just said in an effort to understand why you've suddenly gone quiet. Accompany the pause with a slow scan of the faces in front of you.
- Use a quick pace to convey your excitement or enthusiasm for a topic. If you find a point exciting, let your voice tell the audience so. Use a slow pace with a lower tone and lower volume to convey seriousness or sadness. If you have a solemn message, drop the speed, tone, and volume way down.
- Use volume. Build it up in a crescendo effect as you work through to your most critical point. As you work your way higher, each successive point feels more important than the preceding one. Use volume to express surprise or anger. A suddenly louder statement really gets attention.
- If you want to get attention you can also drop the volume so that the audience has to lean forward to hear you.

Charismatic speakers use the versatility of their voices to drive their messages deep into the emotional parts of their listeners' subconscious. Work hard on polishing and using your voice well.

A great book on developing a "star-like" charismatic voice is *Love Your Voice: Use Your Speaking Voice to Create Success, Self-Confidence, and Star-Like Charisma!* by Roger Love (a successful Hollywood voice coach).

Become a Charismatic Speaker

UK psychologist Professor Richard Wiseman has researched the topic of charisma extensively and finds that charismatic speakers inevitably use all of the communication media they have at their disposal. They use the full range of their voices, support their points with more body language than the uncharismatic, and speak in images as much as possible.

Professor Richard Wiseman summarized his advice to wannabe charismatics approaching a speech or talk:

Be clear, fluent, forceful and articulate, evoke imagery, use an upbeat tempo, occasionally slow for tension or emphasis.

Apply these nine simple techniques and you'll dramatically increase the charismatic impact of your presentations and speeches.

Inspire with Your Vision

13

T HINK OF ANY genuinely charismatic person you've ever met, seen or read about. What is the most outstanding thing about him or her? Vision! Charismatic people have such a clearly developed sense of what they want to achieve, of where they want to go, that they stand out from those around them. This clarity gives them extraordinary focus and enthusiasm for their vision.

[N]othing serves an organization better – especially during these times of agonizing doubts and paralyzing ambiguities – than leadership that knows what it wants (and) communicates those intentions accurately.
— Warren Bennis, founding chairman, Leadership Institute, University of Southern California

Charismatics always have a sort of missionary zeal – a sense that they know exactly what they want and that they'll do whatever it takes to get it.

Adversity Is the Mother of Charisma

In a tough economy one of the first things to go is optimism – closely followed by the ability of many people to pursue their goals. People become frightened and anxious and feel out of control – and when they take their eyes off their goals all they see is doom and gloom.

> Obstacles are those frightful things you see when you take your eyes off your goal.
>
> — Henry Ford, industrialist

Writing in *Inc.* magazine about Apple's famously charismatic leader, Steve Jobs, journalist Steven Bergman observed:

> The major advantage of having Jobs on the job (forgive me) during uncertain and anxious times is his capacity to dispel feelings of ambiguity. With the exception of grief, there is no feeling more emotionally disruptive than the helplessness of not having a sense of direction or purpose in life.

In difficult times a leader who has a clear view of a desirable future, especially someone with the confidence to make that vision a reality, is highly charismatic.

The Appeal of Vision

So many people wander through life with no clear vision of what they want or where they want to go that when they meet someone who has a clear, compelling vision they are immediately attracted to him or her. This response is largely unconscious, which is why people often ascribe magical qualities to those who appear charismatic. They do not realize that they are responding to something they so badly crave for themselves – clarity and vision.

A vision more powerful than your own is a powerful inducement to hand over responsibility to the visionary for thinking about the details of getting from now to the desirable future. That's a huge part of any successful leader's charisma – and that's how a charismatic leader gets results. People first engage with the leader's vision. Then, as a result, they become more fully engaged with their jobs and their organizations than they otherwise would be.

When someone buys into your vision they give you control of their personal GPS and say, "Take me wherever it is you're going."

> A compelling vision drives charisma. Charisma drives engagement.
> Engagement drives results.

Physician, Heal Thyself

In Chapters 3, 4, and 5 we looked at the critical importance of developing a clear direction for yourself in order to create the bedrock of self-confidence that is at the heart of charisma. You cannot instill a confident clarity of vision into others until you have that same clarity yourself.

When you have a clear personal vision, one that is backed up by a set of goals that you are determined to achieve, you are an exception to the vast majority of people. Having clear goals and a clear vision gives you the enthusiasm to get out of bed every day and look forward to the day ahead. Others sense that enthusiasm. They sense an excitement, a clear focus, a mission – and they want in. When you're totally committed to your goals and your own personal mission you absolutely radiate charisma.

Work on yourself first. Be sure that you have a clear, compelling vision for yourself. When you have formulated a clear personal vision you have already raised your charismatic impact. Then you can focus on instilling a vision into others that will make them feel just as enthusiastic, focused, and energetic – and raise your charisma in the process.

You will not successfully give others a clear sense of vision unless you are imbued with one yourself.

The Corporate Vision

Every organization must have a vision – it's an utterly indispensable means of focusing the efforts of the entire organization on a single desirable point in the future. At that point the organization will have achieved what it was established to achieve. The corporate vision is very simply a clear statement of what the organization has committed to becoming in the future.

Great visions are brief, to the point, and easy to understand. They challenge, provide hope for the future, and inspire stakeholders to make the necessary investment to gain something genuinely worthwhile. A clear, compelling corporate vision makes shorter-term goal setting and planning possible.

Entire libraries of books have been written on the topic of creating compelling corporate visions. There is so much powerful literature on the topic that there is no excuse for not having a powerful and compelling vision for your organization.

But creating or adopting a great corporate vision will not automatically make you a charismatic leader. Charismatic leaders are those who have taken a great corporate vision one step further.

The Charismatic Vision

The charismatic leader goes further than simply creating or adopting a good corporate vision. To make that vision maximally attractive to the people who must deliver on it, to make them want to engage with their part in its achievement, the charismatic leader develops a knowledge of the personal needs, goals, and aspirations of each member of his or her team – and then uses that knowledge to customize the corporate vision for each team member. In doing so, the charismatic leader creates a personalized version of the corporate vision in the minds of each of his or her people.

So, although all pull together in the service of a single corporate vision, each person's interpretation of that vision – and what he or she stands to gain from its realization – has been carefully crafted by a charismatic leader to be particularly inspiring for him or her as an individual.

For a vision to be genuinely charismatic for each individual it must:

- Make the work involved important and meaningful, creating a sense of mission.
- Answer the all-important question, "What's in it for me?"

Craft your vision to address the first of these criteria and it's inspiring; craft it to address both and it's charismatic.

> A vision is successful when it "speaks" to a wide audience, tells an engaging story that people want to be a part of, challenges people, and creates a sense of urgency. Success occurs when the vision becomes imbedded in the daily decisions and actions taken of those you want to lead.
>
> — Mark Lipton, author

Making Work Meaningful

We spend most of our waking lives working – so our work defines a lot of the way we feel about ourselves. If we feel that what we do has some greater purpose, contributes to some large and worthy goal, and is genuinely important, then the impact on us is positive. This contributes greatly to higher self-esteem and builds more robust self-confidence. We feel positive and energized.

> People are motivated by a higher purpose and values. Having a purpose that's higher than delivering numbers gives meaning to the work, and unifies an organization.
>
> — A.G. Lafley, former chairman, Procter & Gamble

If we feel that what we are doing has little or no value, or has no significant impact, then it is unavoidable that this sense of worthlessness will leak into our own self-esteem and drain us of optimism, energy and drive.

In a 1961 speech to Congress, US President John F. Kennedy said:

I believe that this nation should commit itself to achieving the goal, before this decade is out, of landing a man on the moon and returning him safely to the

195

earth ... We choose to go to the moon in this decade and do the other things, not because they are easy, but because they are hard, because that goal will serve to organize and measure the best of our energies and skills, because that challenge is one that we are willing to accept, one we are unwilling to postpone, and one which we intend to win, and the others, too.

Rising to the challenge set by Kennedy required the largest commitment of money ($24 billion) ever made by a nation in peacetime. The Apollo program came to employ 400,000 people and was supported by 20,000 universities and business organizations. The rally to develop advanced technologies to support the program would drive American technological advancement for years after the program ended.

In 1975, when computers were still the size of refrigerators, Bill Gates and Paul Allen founded Microsoft with what must have seemed like a ridiculously impossible vision – but it was one that would impact the lives of just about everyone on the planet.

It's said that shortly after joining, Microsoft CEO Steve Ballmer was having second thoughts about the decision. Gates took him to the side and told him he had it wrong. He was thinking about his new position as being a bean counter for a startup, whereas he was, in reality, the first business manager hired to a firm that would put "a computer on every desk and in every home." Ballmer stayed – the first of many great talents that were inspired by this overarching vision. Gates's vision rallied the necessary talent, investment, and enthusiasm to change the world forever.

The message from Kennedy's speech and Gates's inspiring visions? People will rally around a vision that sets bold and even seemingly impossible goals – if those goals appeal to them in terms of their potential impact. Even if the logical part of them says "impossible", the visionary part in them whispers back, "but what if ...?"

Colin Powell, former US Secretary of State, put this perfectly in his book *My American Journey*, when he said, "Make individuals feel important and part of something larger than themselves."

> The greater the discrepancy between the status quo and the vision the more likely people are to attribute charisma to a leader – as long as the vision seems remotely plausible.
>
> — J.A. Conger and R.N. Kanungo, authors

To develop your charisma it is critically important that the vision you share with your people takes account of all of the potential positive impacts its achievement could have on your organization, and even on humanity at large. It is also critical that everyone knows where his or her particular job fits into the vision – why his or her contribution is important to success. Each person must feel that what he or she is doing is critical to the success of the organization; each must see the impact of what he or she does on the vision, the organization, its people, its clients, and its success.

Not everyone can have the same impact on business as Kennedy had on the American nation; not everyone can change the world the way Gates did with Microsoft – but your vision must still have an almost missionary zeal to it. To inspire people with this zeal your vision must suggest a real challenge, a quest to do something difficult, something that will require sacrifice – but something that will be recognized by all around as an extraordinary achievement.

The appeal of the near-impossible is difficult to overestimate – and you see it reflected in the visions of highly successful organizations worldwide. Google wants to "organize the world's information and make it universally accessible and useful," Amazon aims to "build a place where people can come to find and discover anything they might want to buy online," and Apple's vision for itself is to "make a contribution to the world by making tools for the mind that advance humankind."

[T]he idea of doing something that man has never done has great appeal ... one of the reasons we're in the airline business is that I was told it couldn't be done and that it was impossible for a small airline ever to survive.

— Richard Branson, founder, Virgin Group

To be inspiring and charismatic your vision must be larger than life – a real stretch, something that would be a real achievement when complete. For example:

- Becoming the world leader in your field.
- Knocking a seemingly unbeatable top competitor out of the way.
- Changing the entire business model for an industry.
- Changing the way the world does business.
- Changing the lives of everyone on the planet.
- Achieving meteoric growth against incredible odds.
- Being an extraordinary place to work.
- Making incredible profits.
- Creating a brand new business model or technology.

It is critical that the way in which you present your vision to your people makes them feel part of something altogether bigger than any one of them – something that will change the world as they know it. If your vision has sufficient gravitas that even being associated with it is a badge of honor then you're on the right track.

[You] can buy all of the physical things ... you can't buy dedication, devotion, loyalty – the feeling you are participating in a crusade.

— Herb Kelleher, founder, Southwest Airlines

Once you have checked that box then you have already charged your vision with a certain amount of charisma – but not enough. You must also consider a payoff from the realization of your vision that is altogether more personal.

> A leader succeeds only when he or she makes people excited and confident in what comes next.
> — Marcus Buckingham, motivational speaker

What's in It for Me? (WIIFM)

As we mentioned earlier, the charismatic vision is simply the corporate vision interpreted in such a way that for each member of your team there is an almost spiritual payoff coming from the feeling that he or she is working toward something bigger than himself or herself and his or her everyday concerns. But there is also the more temporal payoff that comes from answering the WIIFM concern. It's obvious that people who follow a leader happily and enthusiastically, who find him or her charismatic, are seeing something in that person's view of the world, in that person's vision, that they believe can help them further their own interests.

This explains why someone who is seen as highly charismatic in one situation, with one group of people, can appear dramatically less so to another group of people, or in another situation. Until people know what you can do for them personally a large part of your potential charismatic appeal remains untapped.

As a charismatic leader you must customize the overall vision so that all members of your team see specifically what making the vision come to pass *will mean to them personally* – assuring them that helping you to achieve your vision will help them to achieve theirs.

So if you can identify what constitutes your people's own interests, and if you behave in a manner that helps them to achieve what they want to achieve, you will become more charismatic in their eyes.

It's All about Them

To create a charismatic vision like this you must know all about the goals and aspirations of the people you want to inspire.

Charismatic founder of JetBlue Airways, David Neeleman, underlined the importance of getting close to those you expect to deliver on your promises so that you can personalize your vision for them:

> We have one supervisor for every 80 people. I can't know 7,000 people. But I tell the supervisors, "You can know 80 people. You can know who they're married to, you can know who their kids are, what their challenges are." They know we will deal with their issues, make them feel like there is a personal touch at the company.

To personalize your vision in this manner you need to know more about your people.

- **What are their strengths?**
  And how can you employ those strengths in a way that dramatically bolsters their self-esteem and sense of contribution? How will working toward your vision help them to become even better in their areas of strength?
- **What are their development needs?**
  And how can you help them to overcome any challenges they have in their abilities or skill sets? How can you help them become all they are capable of becoming? Spend your time focusing on making their outstanding strengths even stronger – as opposed to trying to ferret out areas of weakness, which, no matter how much investment you make, will probably never approach the usefulness, to them and you, of their strengths. Make them the best they can possibly be.

- **What goals do they have for themselves?**
  Look at their goals both inside and outside the organization. What do they want to achieve in their lives? Where do they want their careers to take them? How can your vision help them to make their vision come to pass?

- **What does success look like for them?**
  It's the curse of commercial environments that we can tend to assume that most people are equally motivated by financial gain. Certainly, it is important to all – but many people define success in other ways. Until you know the definition of success according to each of your direct reports, then you cannot help them to achieve it. You must know what is important to them. What will make them feel like they have really achieved? It's not the same for everyone.

- **What are their family circumstances?**
  And how do they affect their priorities? How can you harness your vision to give them a vision of a better future for their families and loved ones? Many need to know that they have the necessary security for themselves and their families to survive and thrive no matter what happens. They need to know that you are working to assure them a secure future.

- **What are their passionate interests?**
  Are they doing what they would really passionately like to be doing? If so, how would success in making your vision a reality help them to get even more from their work? If not, how would helping you to realize your vision result in their doing what they *are* passionate about? Can you craft a career for them that they could not get elsewhere?

- **What will they learn from you in pursuing your vision that will help them to realize their own?**
  How will your coaching and mentoring along the way set them up

to target their life's goals more effectively? What do you know that they would like to know – and how can you help them to learn from you? With the exception of feeling like you are engaged in work that will change the world, the next biggest drive for many people is to learn from those whom they consider to be great.

Just being seen to have enough interest in your people to learn what you need to know to do this will make you more charismatic. People will go out of their way to support a leader who takes the time and energy to get to know them more personally and to address their needs as individuals.

The primary way for you to uncover what you need to know about each of your people is through one-on-one conversation and interaction. If you want to engage people charismatically, then you must be prepared to spend time with them – and to make the effort to understand who they are and what's important to them.

To uncover individual strengths, abilities, and development areas, use formal employee assessments. There is no better way to get a really deep insight into an individual's capabilities – many of which will be unknown even to themselves (check out www.profilesinternational.com).

Once you have this insight into each of your people, you are ready to begin to craft a vision that will inspire them to the level of engagement you need to ensure success in making your vision come to pass.

[T]he best way to keep your stars is to know them better than they know themselves ... and then use that information to customize the career of their dreams.

— Timothy Butler and James Waldroop, authors

Communicate Your Vision on Two Levels

So, you've established the two essential dimensions of your charismatic vision – the "big picture" of the potential impact achievement of your vision could have on the world at large, and the more personalized view of each of your people that will allow you to craft a vision for them that is aligned with your overall vision. Now you need to focus on continually "selling" this vision to those you expect to help you make it come to pass.

SALESFORCE.COM

The concept that I like most, and the one I've taken most to heart, is the belief that people cannot be united or focused unless they share a common philosophy – a philosophy that gives their effort greater meaning.

— Marc Benioff, founder, Salesforce.com

First, Sell the "Big Picture" Vision

At a group level, continually communicate the "big picture" significance of your vision. As discussed earlier, people need to belong to something bigger than themselves, and the extent to which you as their leader make them feel this way is the extent to which you are charismatic to them.

Give people work that makes them feel important, valued, and significant; make them feel that they are on a challenging mission, but one they have at least some hope of achieving, and they'll find you charismatic.

In order to sell the big picture, you need to take the following steps:

203

- **Recognize that it begins with you**

  One of the key ways in which charismatic leaders communicate vision is through their day-to-day behavior. People will learn more about your vision from the focused and persistent way in which you pursue it than almost anything else. You must model the values and behaviors you expect your people to display in order to reach your jointly held vision.

  If you're genuinely committed to the vision you're selling, and if that's the way you act in everything you do, then your people will begin to trust that you're serious and will emulate your example – almost regardless of how little you do to formally communicate your vision. As discussed in Chapter 8, emotional contagion will play a large part in causing your actions, moods, and attitudes to be spread throughout your team. Your actions are your best way to communicate your vision and engage people in helping it come to fruition.

  On the other hand, if you are not genuinely committed to the vision you're espousing, you will not be capable of keeping up the pretense. In the absence of this genuine commitment, passion and persistence, your people will not buy into your vision – regardless how much formal communication you use to try to convince them.

- **Start with your opinion leaders**

  In every group there are people who have an above-average influence on the way the group thinks. These opinion leaders – often the future leaders of your organization – are critical to your success in spreading your vision and lighting everyone up with it.

  They must be brought onboard as early as possible – and must be kept onboard every step of the way. Where it's not practical to interact daily with every individual member of your team, even your direct reports, be sure that your opinion leaders are 100 percent onboard. Make them advisers. Actively seek their advice on every step you take to drive toward your vision – especially on how you can position the vision so that it appeals to each member of the team in a more personal way.

Give them ownership of the vision and they'll sell it for you when you cannot be there. Moreover, as trusted colleagues, they will frequently be viewed as more impartial sources of information than you on the positive potential of your vision for all of the team.

- **Celebrate every victory**

However small it is, mark each triumph that takes you closer to achieving the vision. When you celebrate, involve everyone – and be sure that everyone knows just how this victory moved you closer to the vision. Make the vision a living, breathing thing. Actions and behaviors that are celebrated are much more likely to be repeated. Celebrations of victories, however small, have a large impact on behavior.

- **Pass the praise liberally**

Be liberal in your public praise of those who take you closer to achieving the vision in any way, no matter how small. Not only does this motivate the person receiving the praise to strive to repeat his or her success, but it also reinforces the desired behaviors for all other members of the group.

- **Weave the vision into everything**

Communicating your vision needs to be a continuously living process – as opposed to a single annual event like the launch of the new sales year or the annual conference. People need to be fed a diet of your vision on an ongoing basis to ensure that they "get it."

Reference the "big picture" significance of your vision every time you create a new program, new direction, or new goal. Every time you ask people to do something new, be sure that they see what you're asking of them in the context of the overall vision. Then work the vision into every communication: memos, meetings, presentations, internal talks, and speeches. You cannot over-communicate a vision – but it's very easy to under-communicate it.

Continually promote and reinforce the larger significance of your vision and the contribution it will make to all. Ensure that everyone is constantly reminded of the impact they are making on the organization, its employees and clients, and the world at large.

Then, Personalize the Vision

Knowing as much as you now know about each and every one of your people, you have the wherewithal to refine that vision in such a way that it will be meaningful to each of them as individuals. This facet of your vision needs to be communicated one person at a time.

Use your knowledge and insight to align their responsibilities in their current positions so that in striving to achieve your vision they also achieve their own.

On a one-on-one basis:

● **Harness their strengths**
  Give them work that allows their strengths to shine out. Make them obvious top performers in their own eyes and those of their colleagues. Whenever possible, find opportunities and assignments that allow them to indulge their passionate

interests. Once you know what those are you'll find that there are plenty of opportunities to do so.

- **Put them under pressure to be all they can be**
  Provide "stretch" assignments that are critical to the achievement of your vision and other growth opportunities that will help them to realize their own personal career goals. Continually develop their personal value and personal "brand" by helping them to round out their experience and skills through such assignments.

- **Develop them**
  Provide all of the necessary coaching, training, advice, and mentoring to ensure that in following your lead they are developing their abilities, career potential, and personal value at a faster rate than they could anywhere else or in any other way. Be seen to be prepared to provide development that contributes as much, or even more, to their personal vision and goals as it does to their current responsibilities in respect of your vision.

- **Marry their personal vision to yours**
  Map out how what they do along the way to achieving your joint vision will directly move them closer to achieving their personal visions. Show them how the skills they develop, the contacts they establish, the relationships they build, and the experience they gain will all contribute to getting them where they wish to go in a professional or personal sense.

It is critical to recognize that as your people grow and develop, as your vision progresses, then so will their view of themselves, their capabilities and potential – and, as a result, what they wish to do with their lives and careers. So, it is essential that you maintain an ongoing one-on-one dialog that allows you to continually adapt your vision so that it remains consistent with theirs.

If you position yourself as being as interested in your people's success as your own, then you become charismatic and they will positively want to engage with you and their work in a manner that helps you achieve what you need to.

All successful people – men and women – are big dreamers. They imagine what their future could be, ideal in every respect, and then they work every day toward their distant vision, that goal or purpose.

— Brian Tracy, author and speaker

Give Them Clarity and Direction

Clarity of vision is so rare, especially in times of uncertainty, that those who have a clear vision have an unusual appeal.

Think big and aim high. Clarify precisely what you want to achieve – and then enlist your people to your cause. Give them something they can believe in; give them a sense of being on a crusade, of being able to change the world, and then show them how achieving your vision will help them achieve theirs. Give them a mission.

When you become a source of meaning and direction in others' lives you become truly charismatic.

Be Contagiously Energetic and Enthusiastic

14

Y OU'LL OCCASIONALLY MEET some energetic and enthusiastic people who are not charismatic, but you'll never meet a charismatic person who is not energetic and enthusiastic. The charismatic's seemingly boundless energy, the perpetual motion that sees him or her take more decisive action, get more done, and display more enthusiasm than anyone else, is hugely attractive.

Energy and enthusiasm are fundamental elements of charisma. To become charismatic you will need to master them.

Nothing great was ever achieved without enthusiasm.

— Ralph Waldo Emerson, philosopher and poet

The Charismatic Appeal of Enthusiasm

Enthusiasm is like electricity. You cannot see it, but you can see its power and what that power can do. We are all natural conductors of enthusiasm, and when we meet someone brimming with it we are eager to connect and have this life-giving force flow through our minds and bodies.

Speaking with enthusiasm will have an extraordinary effect on any audience. When you're enthusiastic about your topic you can fluff your lines, "um" and "ah" your way through your key points, and screw up your slides – and still make a positive impression. Enthusiasm is persuasive and convincing.

Look what happens when you're with someone enthusiastic. You tune in and immediately start mimicking that person's mood and behavior. You have unconsciously decided that you like what you see and how he or she feels, and you set yourself up to get some of that "feel-good" factor for yourself. Once again, it's the "mood contagion" discussed in Chapter 8.

The Charismatic Equation

The extent to which you are perceived as being charismatic is directly proportional to the extent to which people either feel or fare better after each interaction with you.

Always remember the Charismatic Equation. Your perceived charisma will always be proportional to the value that others take away from interactions with you. If they feel that they are more enthusiastic and energetic after they've met you then they'll come back again and again – you will be charismatic. When you're so infectiously enthusiastic that they find your enthusiasm, energy, and optimism pulsing through their veins after every encounter with you, you become altogether more magnetic.

Everyone is irresistibly attracted to some degree or other by those who emanate energy, enthusiasm, and passion. It is highly contagious. Even one highly optimistic person in a group can change the entire attitude of that group.

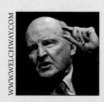

[T]he first essential trait of leadership is positive energy – the capacity to go-go-go with healthy vigor and an upbeat attitude through good times and bad. The second is the ability to energize others, releasing their positive energy, to take any hill.

— Jack Welch, former chairman and CEO, General Electric

When you share your enthusiasm with those around you they become enthusiastic, and they in turn share their enthusiasm with you. Suddenly everyone's buzzing at an even higher level than they were before – and you are the catalyst. This is charisma at its most fundamental.

Your charisma starts with you. Become enthusiastic and your people become energetic and enthusiastic – and your charismatic appeal takes a quantum leap forward.

The Easiest Path to Enthusiasm

The easiest path to genuine enthusiasm is to do something that you love – something that will make a difference that really matters to you. When that's the case then enthusiasm is assured, energy follows, and passion is never far away.

You cannot sustain a genuine, consistent, driving, passionate, and motivated energy in the long term unless you are doing something you love, something you feel passionate about, something you believe in. Charisma is built on the genuine energy and enthusiasm that flows from someone who believes passionately in what he or she is doing. Without that passion it is hard to sustain charisma.

When you're excited about what you're doing you become more animated, energetic, and enthusiastic – and when that happens you become unstoppable. Success is inevitable.

You have to really believe in what you're doing, be passionate enough about it so that you put in the hours and hard work that it takes ... then you'll be successful.

— Pierre Omidyar, founder, eBay

Unless you feel passionate you cannot inspire passion. Find your true passion and you're halfway to the energy and enthusiasm you need to be truly charismatic.

The best way to genuine enthusiasm: do something you love!

Tap Into Your Inner Enthusiasm

Of course, being human, even if you're doing something you're crazy about, there will be days when you find that you're not automatically overflowing with your normal level of enthusiasm. You may be tired or distracted or dealing with a particularly high level of adversity. Those are the days, ironically, when you need the energy of enthusiasm even more. On those days you have to find the wellspring of enthusiasm that is inside of you and consciously tap into it.

The reality is that those who are continually enthusiastic have realized the "secret" of enthusiasm – it is not something automatic. There's no doubt that something you're passionate about will light you up more frequently and more brightly than anything else. But it won't be all the time. Those who have mastered enthusiasm recognize, often subconsciously, that enthusiasm is a choice. If you choose to be enthusiastic you'll be enthusiastic. Act enthusiastically and you'll become more enthusiastic.

On those days when you have to act as if you feel enthusiastic, simply recall a time when you were positively alive with enthusiasm, when you were aware that others around you could feel your passion. Remember that moment and tune into it. Remember what you felt, how you walked, how you spoke – and you'll recover that enthusiasm and tap into the energy it brings with it. With practice you'll find that you're able to turn on your enthusiasm at will, simply by recalling an occasion when you were at your most enthusiastic.

In fact, next time you're brimming with enthusiasm, you should take a few moments to do a quick inventory of how you feel in your body and your mind, how you think, how you walk and speak, how you view challenges and opportunities, and how those around you respond to your enthusiasm. Commit it to memory. That way you'll have that experience to draw on next time you need it. And, with practice, you'll be able to reproduce it at will.

Another great way to build the ability to tap into your natural inner enthusiasm at will is to observe someone who is impressively enthusiastic. Model his or her speech, behavior, language, body language, facial cues, etc. You'll find that the combination of all the things that person does will light the fuse of your internal enthusiasm and it will explode inside you.

You gave up the option of having off days – days when you're not outwardly enthusiastic and energetic – the moment you made your decision to become a leader. You have a responsibility to be enthusiastic – and if you don't feel enthusiastic then act as if you do. That's leadership.

Teach yourself to be enthusiastic at will. That's charisma.

Of course, if you find that you cannot muster any lasting enthusiasm for what you're doing, if it's simply too difficult to create any, then the message is clear: you're wasting yourself. Find something else to do that does fire you up.

CHARLIE BREWER

[Y]ou've got to be passionate about it. I think people that look for great ideas to make money are not nearly as successful as those who say "Okay, what do I really love to do? What am I excited about? What do I know something about? What's kind of interesting and compelling?"

— Michael Dell, founder, Dell Inc.

Enthusiasm Drives Action; Action Drives Charisma and Success

Take two people who have the same skills, abilities, education, and opportunities, but only one has enthusiasm for what he or she is doing. You can be assured that the more successful of the two will be the one brimming with enthusiasm.

Charisma is the transference of enthusiasm.

— Ralph Archbold, speaker

Our research showed that one of the most charismatic things leaders can do is harness their enthusiasm and invest its energy. Charismatic leaders use that energy to take action, refusing to be stunned into inaction by circumstances.

Everything you'll ever read about successful people suggests that they understand a great truth – that things only change and progress through action. So, no matter what the challenges, no matter how grim things look, charismatic leaders are always looking for what they can do in each particular moment that will progress their cause, make things better, make the best use of their time, and further their vision. Charismatics are always proactive.

One of the most important things in sustaining energy is the feeling that you are continually moving forward. A clear vision, clear time-based goals, and a set of daily to-dos that serve those goals are critical elements in this. Each day as you tick off your to-dos and make obvious forward progress, your energy will increase. There is nothing as energizing as the feeling of continually taking action and making positive progress.

Enthusiasm coupled with clear, compelling, and meaningful goals quite naturally creates a tremendous impatience to achieve. This very positively inspired impatience creates passion and pulls on every shred of energy you have in the service of your goals. Suddenly everything becomes positively urgent. You have a sense that time is passing and every moment must be filled with positive action.

Enthusiasm ensures that you're never waiting to see what someone else thinks you should do next. You're already taking the best possible action you can in the moment.

Energy also comes from building a habit of always taking some action in the face of adversity – finding what you can influence in any situation and taking positive, quick action to take control of it.

> The impatience that comes from genuine enthusiasm creates a strong impression of continuous forward-driven motion. It's all action, action, action. And, oh boy, is that ever charismatic.

That combination of enthusiasm, passion, energy, and belief is absolutely irresistible to those around you. Everyone wants to feel that way. As discussed in Chapter 8, they mimic your moods and behaviors so that they can achieve the same unstoppable enthusiasm and energy you radiate. Enthusiastic leaders are naturally charismatic and automatically get much more action and drive from the people who work with them. And that's the secret of their success.

Nurture Your Enthusiasm

Don't leave your enthusiasm to chance. Cultivate and nurture it daily. Here are a few simple ways to do so.

- **Remind yourself of your goals daily**
  Use the Haney-Sirbasku System from Chapter 6 to make this a daily ritual. That way you'll be bolstered by your past successes and enthused by your coming future success – your goals.
- **Revisit your accomplishments daily**
  Nothing will raise your enthusiasm level as much as reviewing your previous successes. This will spark your optimism and

enthusiasm for more success and really rev you up. Again, use the Haney-Sirbasku System to make this part of your daily ritual for getting the day started.

- **Celebrate your successes, big and small**

  Celebrate the successes of those around you – publicly! Celebrate achieving all of your goals, even the small ones, with everyone around you. Every time you hit a goal, "ring the bell" – do something to mark the occasion. Pile praise on those who hit their goals, achieving their part of the overall goal. That way you amplify your enthusiasm and that of all around you and increase everone's energy and thirst for success dramatically.

- **Create a zone of infectious enthusiasm all around you**

  Build everyone else's enthusiasm. Your enthusiasm will feed theirs, theirs will feed yours, and this positive feedback loop will send the level of everyone's enthusiasm through the roof. Every day find a reason to give one or more of the people on your team some positive feedback. Catch them doing something right – and praise them in front of everyone else. Not only will this raise their enthusiasm, but it'll also build their self-worth and position you as a charismatic source of confidence reinforcement for them. When you raise others' enthusiasm you are automatically charismatic.

- **Keep your vision out there**

  People who are eager for the future become enthusiastic. In Chapter 13 you saw how to refine your vision on an ongoing basis, then share it continually with those around you. Not only will it make them impatient for future success, it'll also make them enthusiastic about whatever action needs to be taken to get there. Continually sharing your vision will also reinforce it in your own mind, reminding you what you're striving for – and bolstering your own enthusiasm.

- **Start every day with a clear idea of what you need to achieve that day**

  You have a clear vision and clear goals. Begin each day with a list of to-dos for the day. As you work through them, tick each off the list. When you reach the end of the day, be sure to give yourself a small pat on the back for what you've achieved. This simple ritual gives a real sense of daily achievement and forward movement and builds your enthusiasm for the next day. Take action that moves you forward every day.

  The incredibly efficient electronic systems we all now use to organize ourselves are great, but there is something really satisfying in ticking to-dos off a simple piece of paper – and crumpling the completed list at the end of the day. It provides a great sense of closure.

- **Continually build your knowledge of your business**

  Stay well ahead of all of the trends in your business. Use the expertise-development plan you'll develop in Chapter 16 to stay on top of the newest trends. Not only will your lifelong learning fill you with new and exciting ideas that enthuse you, but your superior knowledge will impress those around you, increase your charisma, and enhance their enthusiasm for working with you. One of Jim Sirbasku's favorite sayings was, "If you're not green and growing, you're ripe and rotting." Stay green; keep growing.

- **Look after your physical energy**

  Exercise is critical in creating a physiological capability for energy. If you already exercise then we don't have to tell you about the difference it makes. If not, then start now – even in a small way. Do a little more each day. Even if you only walk where you once drove, or take the stairs where you previously took an elevator, you're making a difference. Work up to a minimum of an hour of exercise three times a week and you'll see a difference in your energy level – especially if exercise wasn't previously a part of your routine. Get your body fit enough to keep the promises your enthusiastic mind wants to make.

● **Hang out with enthusiastic people**

"Tell me what company you keep and I'll tell you what you are." Cervantes hit the nail on the head! Spend your time with enthusiastic people and your enthusiasm will soar. Pass your time with the patently unenthusiastic and they'll suck you dry of energy, drive, and passion. Seek out those who will feed your enthusiastic self. If you feel your enthusiasm dip, reach out to one of those people. Even a brief conversation with someone enthusiastic can recharge your batteries and get you back on track.

By the same token, limit the time you spend with those who would soak the enthusiasm and energy out of you. Jim Sirbasku used to caution that there were people walking around with psychic umbilical cords, just looking for somebody to plug into. These "energy vampires" have decided not to be enthusiastic, yet they have an endless appetite for your enthusiasm. Ration time with them. Don't let unenthusiastic people drain you.

● **If in doubt, get out**

In a recent survey by Conference Board in the US just 51 percent of people said they were satisfied with their jobs! That means that half the US working population do not like their jobs – and it's probably no different anywhere else in the world. If you don't like your job it will take too much out of you to be enthusiastic about it. Even if you manage to manufacture some enthusiasm in the face of an apathetic or negative attitude to your job, those around you will smell the fake quality of your enthusiasm. "Do what I say, not what I do" will not inspire. In the same survey only 51 percent of people said they were satisfied with their boss – hardly surprising if the bosses are not enthusiastic about *their* jobs.

Microsoft founder Bill Gates said, "What I do best is share my enthusiasm." However, if you don't have it then you obviously cannot share it. If you cannot be enthusiastic about what you're doing then you owe it to yourself – and to your people – to get out and find something to invest your life in that does light your fire. Don't stay in a job that doesn't fit you – it'll kill your spirit. And don't wait for the right time to do something about it. The right time is always now.

The "Holy Trinity" of Charisma

The three behaviors that all charismatic people display continually are energy, enthusiasm, and optimism. These are the very core of charisma – the behavioral foundation for all else you'll do to build yourself the charismatic image you desire. The secret is to recognize that all three can be cultivated.

Enthusiasm is like a mega-affirmation – it sends your mind and body so many positive messages in its expression that it blasts all negativity out of your system and fires you up with the energy you need to do pretty much anything. Enthusiasm trumps anxiety, fear, doubt, and guilt and fosters self-confidence, energy, and happiness.

Dale Carnegie & Associates

A person can accomplish almost anything for which he has unlimited enthusiasm.

— Dale Carnegie,
author and lecturer

For those around you enthusiasm and energy create an aura that is irresistibly magnetic and draws them to you – giving them all the same positive benefits you achieve from it.

Don't suppress it. Release your inner enthusiasm. Decide to be enthusiastic today and take a major step closer to becoming one of those striking charismatic leaders who get extraordinary results from their people.

Be
a Beacon of
Positivity

15

HAVE YOU EVER met anyone charismatic who had a negative outlook? No! And you never will. Optimism is one of those characteristics that is an absolute essential for sustained charisma. This was clearly reflected in our research on charismatic leadership.

No one is attracted to someone who makes them feel less good about themselves or their situation. We don't need anyone's help to feel bad – we can achieve that all on our own if we want to! Charismatic people impact others with the power of their optimism.

The Opposite of a Leader Is a Pessimist

Optimism is not a blind Pollyanna-style refusal to look at the realities of a situation, to ignore harsh realities and to persist with a doomed course of action. Optimism is simply about being open to the possibilities of positive outcomes in any situation – however negative it might at first appear to be.

Optimism is obviously a good feeling. Just looking at the face of an optimistic person tells you that straight away. Optimists positively glow with the positive effects of their disposition. They have endless energy, enthusiasm, and belief in themselves and others – because their focus is always on what could be, on how things will definitely change to get even better in the future.

Get talking with an optimist about the future and he or she will paint you a rich picture of a better time and place – somewhere you'd really like to be, and somewhere you'd most likely be willing to invest a little extra energy into reaching. We all want to be inspired in this way, which is why optimism is so charismatic.

Because of the contagious effects of emotions and moods that we discussed in Chapter 8 – because moods are transmitted from person to person faster than any disease – we all find genuinely optimistic people attractive. Simply being close to them results in our feeling better than we did before we came in contact.

Optimism is particularly essential in a leader, especially one who aspires to being more charismatic. To get people to go that extra mile, to engage with their work much more than the average, you must become a model of what they'd like to be. Marcus Buckingham, the author of *The One Thing You Need to Know: About Managing, Great Leading, and Sustained Individual Success*, said, "The opposite of a leader isn't a follower, the opposite of a leader is a pessimist." Optimism is critical.

Optimists Are More Successful

Quite apart from the inspiring effect that the optimistic have on those around them, all of our research also shows that optimists tend to be more successful.

If you're optimistic then your general outlook is one whereby everything always works out for the best in the end. So, even when things go wrong, you keep pushing forward and taking whatever action you can at that point in time to improve the situation. As mentioned earlier, our research has shown that taking action in the face of adversity is one of those behaviors that people find highly charismatic. After all, if things always work out for the best, then any setback is temporary and there is no good reason for taking your eyes off the prize you have set your sights on.

Optimism is the fuel you burn to create the energy and drive that keeps you moving steadily forward in pursuit of your vision, goal by goal.

This is why optimists tend to be so much more successful than pessimists. Optimists keep moving forward regardless, whereas pessimists, even those every bit as capable as their optimistic peers, fail because they do not persevere. Instead, they crumble under adversity and never reach their real potential.

> No optimism, no fuel. No fuel, no energy. No energy, no drive. No drive, no success.

Optimism and Charisma

So optimists are not only more energetic and enthusiastic, more lively and more driven, but they also tend to be much more successful. Blend together all of those elements and you create the sort of person most people aspire to be.

And, as we said earlier, if you represent something that everyone else wants to be then you are already charismatic. People will seek you out and be willing to follow you. They will find themselves drawn to you unconsciously in the hope that they'll learn your secret – or in the hope that some of your optimism, liveliness, and can-do attitude will rub off on them. By a process of mood contagion they'll model your mood and behavior, and their resulting good feelings will act like a drug that creates a charismatic bond between you and them.

When talking about former US President Ronald Reagan and his charismatic impact on all who met him, Colin Powell, his national security adviser, described his optimism as a "force multiplier" – something that made everything else he did much more impactful.

Optimism Is Practiced

Given the adversity we all face in our challenging lives it is obvious that even the optimist's positive outlook will be challenged on a regular basis. A failure makes everyone question himself or herself from time to time. This is a positive reaction, as long as it doesn't become obsessive. Optimists have a habit of spending much less time than pessimists worrying about setbacks – they bounce back more quickly. This optimism comes as a result of practice – the choice always to select the more positive and optimistic interpretation of anything that happens.

Despite the common expression, no one is really born an optimist. We all learn how to be optimistic or pessimistic at a very early age. Then we practice perfecting whichever of those models we have adopted so that, unless we consciously decide to make a change, our tendencies become more defined and ingrained.

Optimism is a mindset that is forged over time through successive decisions to choose a more positive view of the world. It takes practice.

> Be positive – no matter what situation you find yourself in … never give up. If you're that determined, you'll be much more likely to find something.
> — Richard Branson, founder, Virgin Group

If you're at all pessimistic then it's because you have practiced and refined that mindset. We're not saying that you *chose* to be pessimistic – just that a succession of decisions has resulted in a mindset that does not serve you well. And the good news is that you can change that mindset if you wish.

The Psychology of Optimism

Martin Seligman is a psychologist and director of the Positive Psychology Center at the University of Pennsylvania. He was largely responsible for founding the branch of science known as "positive psychology."

His book *Learned Optimism: How to Change Your Mind and Your Life* is the seminal work on the science behind optimism and on the practical development of a more optimistic outlook. If you haven't already read it, whether you are the most ardent optimist or dyed-in-the-wool pessimist, we highly recommended that you do so – especially given your aspiration to raise your charismatic impact.

How You Explain the World

Seligman identifies the key difference between optimists and pessimists as a difference in "explanatory style" – the way their self-talk explains the things that happen to them.

Pessimism comes from an explanatory style that sees setbacks as events that are likely to have a permanent impact and over which you have no control. Pessimists have a tendency to blame themselves for setbacks they encounter, while good events are viewed are temporary, almost accidental, and unlikely to be repeated. They also take no credit for anything positive that happens to them – fortunate external circumstances caused such happenings.

Anything that goes wrong confirms a pessimist's inner and self-perpetuating sense of a complete lack of control that develops into what Seligman calls "learned helplessness" – a sense of powerlessness that freezes him or her, preventing him or her from taking action that could otherwise change a negative situation so that it has a more positive outcome. The pessimist's explanatory style therefore perpetuates a cycle of self-fulfilling negative prophecies, where helplessness feeds inaction and lack of perseverance, resulting in turn in more setbacks that might well have been avoided by appropriate and timely action.

The cost of not doing anything or inaction is huge. We would rather do something and have an answer, even though it may not be the right one, instead of waiting and not doing anything.
— Meg Whitman, former president and CEO, eBay

Optimists, on the other hand, have an explanatory style that attributes anything good that happens to them as being of their own doing and likely to be permanent in nature. For an optimist, things that are going well will continue to do so in the long term ("Things always work out for the best in the end.") When something bad happens they refuse to believe that they are responsible and find external circumstances to blame. They spend no time beating themselves up over setbacks. They also automatically assume that negative circumstances will change and that any setback can be resolved if they persist in taking appropriate action. Because they persist, even when things become difficult, they tend to be more successful and become more resilient over time.

The optimistic explanatory style explains why optimists tend to be more successful. When things go wrong they take whatever action they can at that point in time to affect the outcome positively. They persist and persevere longer and thereby achieve more desirable outcomes more of the time.

> Pessimism is self-fulfilling. Pessimists don't persist in the face of challenges, and therefore fail more frequently even when success is attainable … their explanatory style now converts the predicted setback into a disaster, and disaster into a catastrophe.
>
> — Martin Seligman, psychologist

Pessimism Can Be Unlearned, Optimism Can Be Learned

Your explanatory style was learned from those around you as you grew and matured. You absorbed the explanatory style of those closest to you – your parents and those others who played a key role in your upbringing. Then, having acquired this explanatory style at an early stage, you spent the rest of your life proving that your explanatory style is accurate, reinforcing it. The good news is that, just as a pessimistic explanatory style and the resulting helplessness was learned, it can equally be unlearned.

Seligman lays out a step-by-step approach to achieving this. It includes approaches like:

- Practicing becoming aware of your thoughts in the face of adversity, and observing the effects of those thoughts on your responses.

- Writing down negative thoughts and scheduling a later time to consider them when you will expect you'll be better able to objectively assess them – when the initial impact of setback has passed.
- Distracting yourself from a negative spiral by focusing on something else.
- Arguing forcefully and logically with yourself against a tendency to see nothing but the worst in every situation in order to recognize the temporary nature of each setback.

Optimism is such an essential element in charisma that we recommend that, if you have any tendency toward pessimism at all, you should read Seligman's book for a more detailed discussion.

Hone Your Optimism

Even if you're fundamentally optimistic, there are things you can do to reinforce your optimism and to strengthen it so that it is capable of sustaining you even in the most trying and difficult of circumstances.

Here are a few suggestions of practices for doing so:

- **Work on your self-talk**
  If you're already pretty optimistic then continually reinforce that view of yourself through your affirmations. Continually remind yourself that this is how you want to be. Work on refining that mindset even more.

  If you're inclined to be more pessimistic, start using the affirmations to replace your practiced negative self-talk, explanatory style and self-image with that of an optimist. Start planting those seeds. Use the affirmations approach discussed in Chapter 5 to start this transformation.

- **Stay focused on your goals**

  "Obstacles are those frightful things you see when you take your eyes off your goal." Henry Ford's famous saying absolutely nails one of the key elements in maintaining optimism – compelling personal goals. Because they give you a clear direction, goals make you feel good about the present moment and counteract a negative explanatory style by focusing your mind on a positive outcome you are continually moving toward. Make sure that you have a compelling set of personal goals, not just goals for your business (see Chapter 3). Doing so assures you that you are continuing to grow, develop and move forward, regardless of what happens to you professionally. You always have a clear picture in front of you of where you're going, so that setbacks are only temporary blips along the way.

- **Find positive people to spend your time with**

  Seek out the most optimistic people you can find – and spend time with them. Again, mood contagion and observation will both reinforce your own optimism and allow you to observe the ways in which others bolster their own optimism. You'll find yourself adopting their positive attitudes and habits, and you'll always come away refreshed after drinking from someone else's optimistic reserves. When you get a challenge that threatens to dent your optimism, call one of these people. Even talking to them on an unrelated topic will buoy you up again as you absorb some of their optimism.

- **Read inspirational literature**

  In the expertise-development strategy you'll develop in the next chapter, build in a goal to become an expert on yourself and your psychological development. Start with Seligman's *Learned Optimism*, and keep your eyes out for other books and recordings that take different approaches to helping you raise your level of optimism and improve yourself. It's said that you are what you eat. You are also what you read and absorb into your mind. Feed your mind a positive diet and you'll become more positive and more able to see possibilities – especially in difficult situations. Feed your mind a junk diet of negativity and worry and you'll become mentally flabby and lethargic. Optimism energizes and vitalizes. Feed your mind.

- **Tune out negative people and sources**
  Naturally you will not be able to completely cut yourself off from all of those people in your life who are stuck with a pessimistic outlook and are looking for others to bring down to their level of pessimism with their negative talk. But you can choose to limit your exposure. You can also choose not to empathize with or internalize negative sentiments. Do not expose yourself to negativity unnecessarily – it takes energy to overcome. Use that energy elsewhere.

- **Look for the opportunity to take action**
  Optimists see opportunities in every catastrophe, pessimists see catastrophes in every opportunity. When you experience a negative setback, don't allow your self-explanation to hijack your optimism.

  In *How to Stop Worrying and Start Living*, Dale Carnegie suggests that you acknowledge any setback and consider what the worst possible outcome might be. When you've done that, stop and think, "What is the best thing I can do right now that will have the positive effect of moving me even a fraction away from that worst possible outcome?" Take that action. Then repeat the process – always take some action in the face of adversity. Don't allow setbacks to paralyze you. Any positive action that moves you forward, however little, is preferable to none at all – and the ability to take such action is highly charismatic.

- **Acknowledge your achievements**

  When things get tough and any self-doubt slips in, take out the Haney-Sirbasku System discussed in Chapter 6 and revisit the "Accomplishments" section. Read through them carefully and remind yourself of how accomplished you really are. Look at all of the things that you have achieved and use the confidence this builds to keep you focused regardless of adversity. These accomplishments did not come about by accident – you made them happen. Acknowledge this and you reinforce a more positive explanatory style. Shore up your self-belief.

- **Dress and groom yourself well**

  When optimism is dented and pessimism starts to creep in it is often accompanied by a lethargy that robs you of your interest in attending to seemingly small things like this. When you suffer a setback that dents your self-esteem or knocks you back, then respond by dressing yourself in whatever clothing makes you feel most confident and empowered. Get your hair cut; get a massage; put on your best outfit. Your appearance sends your mind strong messages on how you should feel. Look good and you'll feel better.

- **Get lots of rest and exercise**

  Optimism takes energy, especially in times of challenge or adversity, and the best way to get this energy is by ensuring that you get enough sleep and exercise. Exercise not only has the very positive effect of releasing endorphins that give you a lift and automatically dispose you to a more positive frame of mind, but it also gives your body the stamina to deal with the mental demands you'll naturally encounter from day to day.

"Leaders Are Dealers in Hope"

This is as true today as it was when Napoleon Bonaparte first said it. You must become a purveyor of optimism, of hope, of a vision of a much better future.

Once you imbue your people with optimism, the energy and enthusiasm you want to instill in them for your shared vision becomes altogether easier to ignite in the manner we discussed in the last chapter. When you can make people optimistic, energetic, and enthusiastic you are truly a charismatic leader.

Be *the* Expert in Your Field

16

As you can read in Appendix I, our research demonstrated that employees found leaders who were focused on their own personal development charismatic. Those leaders who displayed a clear commitment to their own ongoing development, who continually sought to improve themselves and their knowledge, were more charismatic than those who did not.

That research also showed that leaders who appeared creative – approaching their jobs with imagination and originality, taking bold, calculated risks, or inspiring innovation – were also highly charismatic. There is undoubtedly a certain creative spark that some people have and others don't, but knowledge and a high level of expertise can go a long way to enabling any leader to be much more creative – and therefore charismatic – in the eyes of his or her people.

This was pretty much as we had expected. All of the existing charisma research we reviewed before we started our own study indicated that a very common attribute of charismatic people is an expert reputation. Those with a charismatic persona are generally viewed as having above-average expertise or ability in some key area that is of interest to those who find them charismatic.

It's easy to see why others would find expertise attractive. We'd all like to perform at above-average levels and the opportunity either to learn from people who do, or even just to be associated with them and the results they achieve, makes them attractive. Expertise is a common component of charisma.

Before we look at how you can build a reputation as an expert, let's first define an expert – in what some might think are somewhat cynical terms. For our purposes an expert is simply someone who is seen to know more than the majority of people on any topic. So to be an expert you do not have to know everything about your chosen topic, just more than the majority of people around you.

> You do not have to be a genius to become an expert. You just need to work a little harder than anyone else at doing so.

So how do you become an expert? Two basic steps …

First Step: Develop Your Expertise Continually

How do you achieve this? Read. It's that simple. Almost everyone around you tells themselves that they no longer have the time to read as much as they'd like (though the reality is that they've just made something else a higher priority). If you wish to build expert power you need to read much more than anyone else on your topic. Stay on top of your industry, read widely, and educate yourself so that you are as up to date as anyone can be on developments in your industry or profession.

CHARLIE BREWER

> Read books. Read websites. Read other people. Circle the pitfalls and highlight the opportunities. Then build a vision of how it all could be better and work like hell to make it happen.
>
> — Michael Dell, founder, Dell Inc.

If yours is a broad-ranging profession then select a strategically important slice of that industry to focus on. Pick the topic that is of most critical importance to whomever it is you'd like to find you charismatic. Remember, charisma is about others' perceptions. Make it a goal to become *the* authority on that segment – first in your immediate group, then in your organization, afterward in your region, then in your country – and, ultimately, in the world.

Focus on those books that specifically address the newest developments in your field, the most innovative new approaches to addressing the key challenges in the target segment of your profession or business. The more you study the latest trends and developments in your field, the greater the distance you put between yourself and your peers. Most people learn about new developments third or fourth hand. By reading the latest works in your field before your peers you steal a march on most people you'll encounter.

Set a goal of reading one of these books per week. That's 50 books per year. Your reading rate will increase with practice, but it takes 30–60 minutes per day, six to seven days per week to read a typical book.

Buy your books monthly and take the time to select the four or five each month that are the freshest and most relevant available at that point in time.

E-Book Readers

We strongly recommend e-book readers (e.g., the Amazon Kindle, the Barnes & Noble Nook, or the Sony Reader) as an aid to this objective. With these excellent devices you get instant online access to just about any decent new book that hits the market.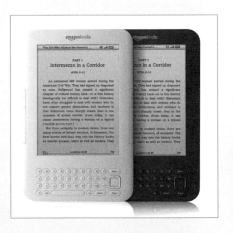
Not only do you have instant access, but the books also tend to be less expensive than their paper counterparts (especially when you factor in the cost of shipping or the time to go book shopping).

Most e-book readers also have also a very nifty feature that allows you to highlight passages in the books you read, and even add your own notes – with a view to later exporting those passages for use in your word processor, for example.

A great investment.

Second Step: Build Your Expert Reputation

Look at where you will be at the end of the first month if you implement this simple strategy. You will already have read four to five of the freshest publications in your field. You will already be way ahead of the vast majority of your peers.

But reading is not enough. In order to build a reputation, you've got to share your newfound expertise. It's not enough to be an expert. You must also let people know that you have this expertise. This is no time to be modest.

As you read your first four or five books, your mind will be subconsciously thinking about all the ways your new learning can be applied to what you do – how you could improve all aspects of your work or business. You'll find that you'll be highlighting passages and taking notes as your creative juices start to flow more freely than ever before.

Get Writing

Now write at least one article on whatever you think is the best application of whatever you learn each month. We are not talking about writing a book review – that only publicizes the author's expertise. No, take what you have learned from your reading and use that newfound knowledge to write a piece of your own that will make it easy for others to apply what you've just learned. Give them your particular take on how this newfound knowledge can improve their businesses. If your article saves them from reading those four or five books, then your job is done. You are now their source of expertise, and you're well on the road to being perceived as an expert.

As you read this you may be thinking, "I'm not much of a writer" or "I don't have time to write an article a month." Don't let that obstacle get in your way. Sketch out the key ideas you want to communicate in your articles and then commission a ghostwriter. There are tens of thousands of freelance writers, experts in every conceivable field, available for hire on www.elance.com, www.guru.com and other sites like those – and the costs are extremely competitive. As long as you have the newfound knowledge you can harness article writing to build your expert reputation.

> In an age when it is easier to be published than ever before it is amazing that people are still inordinately impressed by anyone who has been. Leverage that fact.

Now Share Your Expertise

When you have your article, do one or all of the following:

1. **Create your own blog and publish your article online**

   This exposes your work to an enormous potential audience and will ultimately get you into daily contact with others in your field who are interested in the same topics as you. Those others may have even more expertise, which they'll be anxious to share with you (which will raise your expertise in turn). Buy a good book on how to promote your blog, or just run an Internet search for "promote your blog" (at the time of writing we did so and we got 43 million hits for pages that mention that phrase!).

   Now you have a private publicity platform and, over time, you'll have an audience. Promote your blog in your e-mail signature, on your business card, and on the end of anything else you publish.

   Don't have time? Again, look to www.elance.com and www.guru.com for freelance help. Farm out anything you can't directly handle yourself. It's still your ideas and thoughts that will drive the blog – and your reputation that will be enhanced by it.

2. **Submit your article to any industry/professional publications that cover your field**

   Editors are always on the lookout for fresh material for their magazines and online resource sites. Don't look to get paid – that limits the number of people who'll take your piece, and the amount you get will not usually justify the effort you go to in writing the piece anyway. You are in the business of promoting your expertise, not being a low-paid amateur author. Your payoff is the boost to your profile and reputation. Insist that anything that is published carries your name and a one- or two-line biography, with contact information if possible.

3. **Submit your article to as many online article resources as possible**
   There are literally hundreds of article sites that provide articles to all sorts of paper-based and e-publications, newsletters, webmasters, and so on. Search the Internet for "free article sites" and you'll get all you can handle. Make it a condition that all of your articles are used only in unedited form and only when they are accompanied by your full details: your name, a brief biography, and contact details. With these services be sure to express your copyright to avoid confusion.

4. **Turn your article into a presentation or briefing**
   This could be as short as 20 minutes or as long as one hour. Offer this briefing to your direct reports and other colleagues as a seminar or webinar (if a webinar then record it for future distribution via your blog or personal website).

   Be sure to offer to present it to your clients and prospective clients too.

   Also offer to present it to the organizations and professional bodies who represent your business or profession, or to professional associations who represent your target clients.

Payback Time

Now look at where this simple strategy will have gotten you by the end of the first month.

- You are four or five books ahead of your peers in terms of your understanding of trends and developments in your field.
- You have a valuable article that will become an ambassador, carrying your name far and wide both offline and online.
- You have presented a briefing to at least one group (and perhaps

recorded the briefing for future distribution and publicity use).

- You have planted an article in your blog and/or on article sites that will remain "open for business" forever. Once your piece goes on the web it will get a life of its own and travel the world. Your name will travel with it.

After just one month it is clear that you will already have moved closer to being an genuine expert in your field, but, just as importantly, you have also substantially raised people's *perception* of you as an expert.

Rinse and Repeat

So, now do it again in month two, three, four …

Look forward a year into your program and see what you will have achieved.

- You will have read 50 books – which puts you 50 books ahead of most of your peers.
- You will know far more about your chosen subject than the majority of people you encounter and just as much as the rest.
- You'll have written twelve articles – twelve written ambassadors that will carry your name to every corner of your organization, every corner of your industry, every corner of the world – and you will have developed a reputation as an authority for the thousands of visitors you attract to your blog.
- You'll have twelve months of traffic and discussion on your blog (and all of the expertise development that this brings with it).
- You'll have delivered some briefings and raised your profile inside your organization and elsewhere.

- You'll be starting to get e-mails and calls from journalists looking to pick your brain on your expert topic – and quoting you in their pieces.
- Between the content of your blog and your articles you may find you have the foundation of a book – another prestige builder.

Not only are you very quickly becoming an expert but, just as importantly, you are *seen* to be becoming an expert. You are building a robust expert reputation. According to Dr Donald E. Wetmore of the Productivity Institute, 95 percent of the books in the US are purchased by 5 percent of the population. It is not much different elsewhere. The old adage that "readers are leaders" has never been more accurate. Push your reading beyond the average even of that select 5 percent and you push yourself into a very select group indeed.

What Is the One Thing that Might Stop You Doing This?

You're pushed for time, right?

Of course you're busy – and the biggest challenge *is* finding the time. There's no denying it – we are all busier than ever before. That's why the first thing you have to do is make a commitment that you are going to find that time. Make it one of your goals. Then start looking for ways to achieve it. Build it into your visualizations and you'll find that somehow the required time becomes available. Your RAS will take care of that (see Chapter 4).

Thirty minutes of reading in bed last thing at night is a great way of killing two birds with one stone – winding down a little and getting ready to sleep, while also getting some of your targeted reading done.

Think of all of the obvious times when you might be able to recycle time in the same manner as we discussed in Chapter 4. If you ever travel by plane or train, you can obviously harness some of that time. If you travel primarily by car, then use audiobooks. You can get just about every major title on audio these days (check out www.audible.com, for example).

Finally, if you really cannot carve out sufficient time to read your target number of books, simply halve the workload. Follow exactly the same program – but instead of one book per week aim for two per month. The results will all be halved, but you'll still be ahead of the majority of people around you in terms of your knowledge of your specialist area and the rise of your expert reputation.

Whatever else you do, be sure to set a goal for the number of books you'll read monthly. Otherwise, it will simply fall away.

Leverage the Charismatic Power of Expertise

Commit to this program and just one month from now you will notice yourself pulling away from your peers in terms of your expertise in your specialist area. Twelve months from now you will have a dramatically higher level of expertise and a serious reputation as someone who is well above the average. Five years from now – well, the sky's the limit.

Make it a priority and you'll find the time. Be an expert – be more charismatic.

The Charismatic
Power of Belief
in People

17

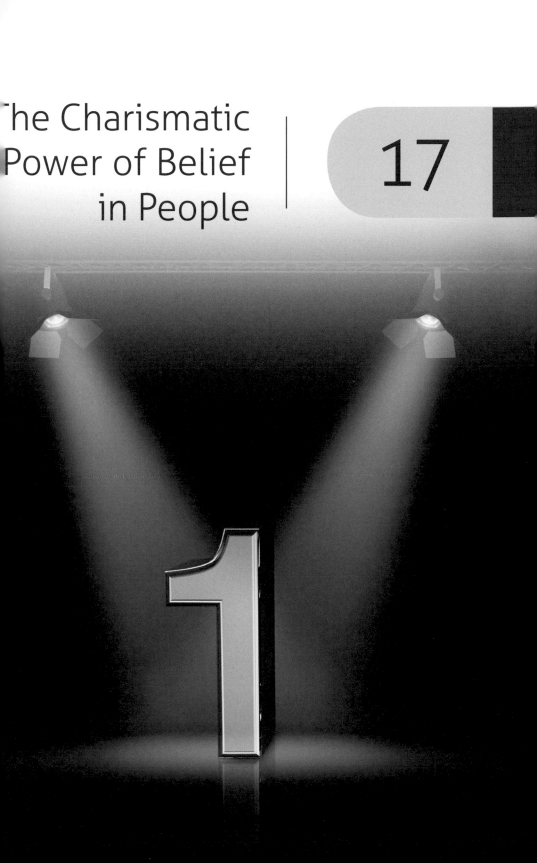

A S WE MENTIONED earlier when we spoke about the Charismatic Equation, the extent to which you are seen as charismatic is largely the extent to which people feel or fare better after each encounter with you. If after every meeting or interaction with you their mood or self-esteem is raised, or their ability to perform is increased, then to them you are charismatic.

As a leader wishing to harness charisma in the service of your organization your challenge is not only to make your people feel and fare better personally but also to harness those more positive feelings to produce behaviors that achieve a superior contribution to the organization.

If you can create an environment where people notice that their self-esteem rises when they interact with you, if they realize that they become capable of much more when working for you than when working alone or for anyone else, if they find that their expectations of themselves and their belief in their own abilities are higher as a result of spending time with you, then you become a genuinely charismatic leader. Your charisma drives employee engagement and the superior performance and contribution that comes with it.

Pygmalion and Galatea – the Myth

Pygmalion was a master sculptor in Greek mythology. Disillusioned by real women, he determined to create a sculpture of a perfect woman in marble. He named his beautiful flawless female figure Galatea. Pygmalion fell completely in love with Galatea and would dress her in the finest clothes, adorn her with the finest jewelry, and bring her grand gifts. His love was so impressive that the Greek goddess of love, Aphrodite, took pity on him and brought Galatea to life.

The beliefs and expectations of the perfect woman that Pygmalion had sculpted into Galatea were brought to life. All of his expectations of his perfect companion were fulfilled in reality and Pygmalion and Galatea fell deeply in love. According to the myth, they lived, well, happily ever after.

Pygmalion and Galatea could never have guessed that, thousands of years later, their tale would be cited as critical to the success of leaders who aspire to exert a charismatic influence on the results their people produce.

> Outstanding leaders go out of their way to boost the self-esteem of their personnel. If people believe in themselves, it's amazing what they can accomplish.
>
> — Sam Walton, founder, Wal-Mart

Pygmalion and Galatea – in Real Life

In his worldwide 1936 book *How to Win Friends and Influence People* (still a worldwide bestseller today), Dale Carnegie counseled that to be a leader who gets the very best results from people you should "Give the other person a fine reputation to live up to." Carnegie observed or sensed the critical impact that leader expectations have on follower performance.

In 1968 a study by researcher Dr Robert Rosenthal showed the impact that others' expectations have on performance. Teachers were given a list of students whom they were told had achieved exceptionally high results on IQ tests, indicating extraordinary ability. This set the teachers' expectations of those students higher than for other students in their groups. In reality, that list of students was selected completely randomly. As a group they had no higher ability than would be expected of any other randomly selected group of students. No one ever told the children that they were considered high performers. Nonetheless, they received this message through their teachers' nonverbal cues like facial expressions, touch, and gestures and through other, more overt, behaviors that communicated their expectations. After just eight months the "high-ability" students were scoring consistently higher than other students in the group.

Since then dozens of studies from around the world have shown the dramatic impact on performance of leader expectations in a wide variety of commercial environments. In his *Harvard Business Review* article entitled "Pygmalion in Management," Professor J. Sterling Livingstone of Harvard Business School observed from his research that "The way managers treat their subordinates is subtly influenced by what they expect of them." One of the most prolific researchers of this effect is Professor Dov Eden of Tel Aviv University. According to him:

> [E]xperimental research has replicated this phenomenon among adult supervisors and subordinates in a variety of military, business, and industrial organizations and among all gender combinations. Both men and women lead both men and women to greater success when they expect more of them.

The power of expectations in driving superior performance is encapsulated in two principles that are critically important to anyone aspiring to be a charismatic leader – the "Pygmalion effect" and the "Galatea effect."

The Pygmalion Effect

The Pygmalion effect is all about the expectations you, as a leader, have of your people.

Consciously or unconsciously you have formed opinions, impressions and expectations of every person in your group. Whether you like it or not, you continually and unconsciously transmit those expectations to all around you through behavioral, verbal, and nonverbal cues. Dov Eden's research shows that, when leaders expect more of someone, they are quite naturally more likely to consciously provide additional input, feedback, and encouragement. However, it has also shown that they tend unconsciously to exhibit more of the positive and encouraging nonverbal behaviors discussed in Step 3 – nodding positively more, smiling more, maintaining longer eye contact, and generally displaying more patience for those of whom they have high expectations.

As discussed in the section on physical charisma, we are all highly skilled at picking up such nonverbal cues. Through the process of emotional contagion, we even tend to mirror the feelings and emotions of those transmitting them.

The upshot is that we strive to perform in accordance with the expectations of those who lead us. If, as a leader, your expectations are consistently positive and high, then your people's self-esteem is consistently raised and they are much more likely to engage positively in an attempt to deliver performance consistent with your expectations.

The leader who has a high level of belief in his people and high expectations of them is like Pygmalion – sculpting an image of exactly what he perceives as most desirable.

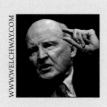

WWW.WELCHWAY.COM

The way to get faster, more productive, and more competitive is to unleash the energy and intelligence and raw self-confidence of the American worker.

— Jack Welch, former chairman, General Electric

Those who seek to get the engagement and productivity that charismatic leaders get from their people must be aware that having lower-order expectations of people is not good business. If your expectations of your people are low, and regardless of whether you overtly communicate them or not, then they are less likely to strive to reach any level of notable performance. Research shows that people are just as likely to strive to "live down" to a leader's low expectations of them as they are to attempt to live up to high leader expectations.

Equally, having moderate or even higher-order expectations that go unexpressed is counterproductive too. Think of the effect of a charismatic leader's failing to recognize the contribution of one team member as frequently as he or she recognizes another's. This can have exactly the same effect on that individual as having low expectations.

Bottom line: if you have positive expectations of all of your people then, consciously and unconsciously, you will continually transmit those expectations and support your people in raising their self-esteem, their expectations of themselves, and their engagement with their work to produce the results you expect of them.

This is the Pygmalion effect. A leader who harnesses this effect creates in his or her people the belief that they are capable of great achievement and success. People come to have the beliefs of their capabilities and performance that their leaders promote to them – for positive or negative.

The Pygmalion effect is important because of this impact. But it is also important because it kicks off something even more powerful that must be harnessed by any aspiring charismatic leader – the Galatea effect.

Our business is based on faith in the value of human potential.

— George Zimmer,
founder, Men's Wearhouse

The Galatea Effect

The Galatea effect says that people's expectations of themselves and their opinions of their capabilities are the greatest determinants of their actual performance.

When a leader cultivates a genuine belief in the ability of all of his or her people to achieve at a much higher level than they do now, or even at a higher level than they previously believed they could, then he or she automatically raises those people's views of themselves – their self-esteem. Those who are led by a leader who consistently expects the very best of them find their self-esteem rises continually, and so they begin to believe that they are capable of much more than they previously had.

Because their self-esteem begins to rise they find that, when they hit obstacles en route to more demanding goals, they are much more likely to persist and push through to success. Because they believe that they can achieve what is expected of them, their actions reflect that belief, resulting in behavior that gets the desired results. This in turn further justifies the same self-belief. This self-fulfilling prophecy of self-imposed expectations is called the Galatea effect.

As a charismatic leader it is your role to believe in your people so fully, and to form such high expectations of them, that they come to believe in themselves and their abilities and thereby raise their expectations of themselves.

Your expectations of success become their expectations, and their expectations allow them to drive consistently for greater success. And if they believe they can succeed then they are very likely to do so. The Galatea effect is a natural result of a leader's employing the Pygmalion effect.

Leadership is communicating to people their worth and potential so clearly that the come to see it in themselves.
— Stephen Covey, author

Pygmalion, Galatea and Charisma
A key element in building a charismatic *and* productive relationship with your

people, one that positively engages them with their work and achieves superior results, is enabling the Pygmalion and Galatea effects.

First you must get the Pygmalion effect in action – and that will bootstrap the Galatea effect. Once the Galatea effect is taking off, all you need to do is accelerate it – and the level of engagement and performance of your people will soar.

Because this increased self-esteem, extraordinary performance and accelerated self-development stems from you, your team members will begin to see you in a charismatic light. Interestingly, as an increasingly charismatic leader your ever-more-respected expectations will have even more impact on them, perpetuating and accelerating the cycle.

Applying Pygmalion and Galatea: A Critical Belief Challenge

The Pygmalion effect is all about building self-esteem and confidence in your people through a process of exposing them to your high expectations of their capabilities. Your first goal should be to continually build their belief in themselves and their capabilities on a daily basis.

In some ways this is easier if you are coming to a brand new team. In that situation you have no preconceived notions and have developed no particular expectations of your people, either positive or negative. Retroactively applying this approach in an even-handed manner across every member of a team you've worked with for some time presents more of a challenge. You will have already made conscious or unconscious decisions as to the ability of each member of your team. For those you have identified as having potential there is no problem, but for those you have (even unconsciously) written off, you will be required to make some changes in your beliefs in order to get the best of them.

Ask yourself honestly: do you believe that everyone has something to offer – and recognize that most people never meet their potential simply because no one was prepared to set high expectations for them and then hold them responsible for living up to them? If not, then you have a task ahead: to become a charismatic leader, you need to make this one of your core beliefs.

It is important to recognize that most people have too little faith in themselves and what they are capable of – and it is this low self-expectation that sets the level at which they perform. They will perform at the level at which you have judge their potential to be. Even your best people are unlikely to have a self-expectation as high as their real potential.

Self-confidence is not the real secret of leadership. The more essential ingredient is confidence in other people. Leadership involves motivating others to their finest efforts and channeling those efforts in a coherent direction. Leaders must believe that they can count on other people to come through.

— Rosabeth Moss Kanter, professor in business, Harvard Business School

To make these motivational tools work you must decide that you are going to start approaching every member of your team with the open attitude that they are all capable of something great – but that their greatness just needs to be uncovered, exposed to themselves, and then nurtured by you through a process of expectation. Make the decision that you will find what every one of your people is capable of, and then instill into them the highest possible expectations of themselves. Quite apart from positioning you to make the Pygmalion and Galatea effects work for your team, this obvious optimistic expectation of the best in others is in itself a charismatic act. It will attract people to you in an almost magnetic sense. We all need someone to see our potential clearly enough to point it out to us.

Start the process by harnessing the Pygmalion effect.

Harnessing the Pygmalion Effect

The entire cycle begins with the raising of positive expectations to initiate the Pygmalion effect in each one of your direct reports.

Some key actions you can take:

- Be aware of your nonverbal cues and ensure that your language, gestures, facial expressions, and general body language are positive and encouraging. Chapters 7–11 tell you precisely how to model the sort of positive and encouraging nonverbal communication that is required here.
- Work with all team members to establish goals that challenge them, providing encouragement and support by showing them you are confident that they can achieve those goals.

  Be careful, however. Creating too high an expectation too early in the cycle can be intimidating and can short-circuit the entire process. Interestingly, research shows that goals set too low, so that they are almost certainties, have an equally negative impact. Ensure that goals require a real stretch, but that both parties see them as achievable. Better to encourage your team with a series of small successful goals than to risk the impact of one major failure.
- Arrange formal opportunities to spend time with each of your people and, when you are with them, be with them 100 percent. Give each person your entire attention, focusing on your expectations of him or her and how you can work together

to make them come to pass.

- Give your people projects or training that builds on existing strengths and develops new skills that will help them do what you expect of them more efficiently.

- Provide regular, supportive one-on-one feedback that recognizes when things go right and provides positive assistance to get back on track when things go awry.

- Provide individualized and public praise for every positive step forward in striving to meet the expectations put upon them.

- Look for their feedback on both your expectations and their progress against them. Let them talk. You listen.

- Show unshakable optimism in their capability to succeed. Do not agree with them if they cannot immediately see their own capabilities. Remain completely positive about your confidence in them (besides anything else, showing such optimism in another is highly charismatic).

Bolstered by the necessary support and assistance in reaching their goals, and by a series of successes, your positive expectations will be transferred to each of your people, developing their self-esteem and self-belief.

ONINNOVATION

We believe that people are basically good, we believe that everyone has something to offer, we believe that an honest, open environment can bring out the best in people, we recognize everyone as an individual, we encourage you to treat others the way you want to be treated.

— Pierre Omidyar, founder, eBay

Your team's enhanced belief in their own capabilities will lead quite naturally to higher expectations of themselves and set the stage for them to harness the Galatea effect.

Harnessing the Galatea Effect

Remember that individuals' expectations of themselves and their opinions of their capabilities are the greatest determinants of their actual performance. This is the Galatea effect.

Through a consistent and deliberate process of imbuing your team with your positive expectations of them, each member will develop ever-higher expectations of himself or herself over time. As this occurs, your focus should turn to fostering the Galatea effect, which will allow them to achieve even more.

Do this through a process of support, encouragement and persuasion that continually builds their self-belief and expectations.

Use approaches like:

- Providing progressively more challenging assignments that require team members to stretch themselves more and more all the time. Give them an opportunity to exercise their own self-expectations by pushing though difficulties encountered in the pursuit of more challenging goals.
- Providing opportunities to work with others who are seen as successful in the areas where you expect them to excel. Pierre Omidyar, the charismatic founder of eBay, made this a core principle. His simple policy was, "Empower others to be experts in what they do and then step back."
- Providing continual feedback and recognition of successes. External recognition from a respected leader bolsters internal

self-esteem, which raises self-expectation and drives the Galatea effect even harder.

- Providing lots of opportunities for public recognition upon successful completion of particularly challenging assignments. Be lavish in your praise of success and progress. However, do not provide praise and recognition unless it is genuinely warranted.
- Getting to know every one of your people inside out, as discussed in Chapter 13. Uncover the particular strengths of each and provide challenging assignments that enhance those strengths.

A.G. Lafley, the charismatic former CEO of Procter & Gamble, made this his mission:

> I know the top 500 people in the company and I am personally involved in career planning for the 150 who are potential presidents or function heads. I review their assignment plans at least annually, assess their strengths and weaknesses ... Little if anything else I can do as CEO will have as enduring an effect on P&G's long-term future.

Focus on enhancing strengths that will have maximum impact on your people's performance and success. In this way you will enhance your team's expectations of themselves even further.

- Knowing each of your people well enough that you have a clear insight into their work and work-aligned interests – the sorts of activities that passionately motivate them – again, as discussed in Chapter 13. Harness the additional motivation of those passionate interests by providing even more challenging tasks in those areas.
- Making clear your personal commitment to giving your team all

of the help, support, coaching, information, and resources they need to succeed.

- Being sure that you share all of the information that you can in order to help your people be successful. Keep them completely informed.
- Assigning each team member a successful mentor – someone who represents the expectations you have of each person, to provide advice and guidance as required.

There Is Nothing More Charismatic than Positive Expectation

In Chapter 15 we spoke about the charismatic impact of optimism. The finest expression of charismatic optimism is an unshakable and highly visible belief in the capabilities of others to achieve great things. As a charismatic leader you must have the very highest expectations of your people, knowing that your expectations will become their expectations   and that their expectations will translate to unprecedented productivity, performance, and success.

When people see what they are capable of when working for you, they will positively want to work for you in helping you achieve what you are striving to achieve. And you'll you truly possess charisma of the type we defined in Chapter 1: "a special quality of leadership that captures the popular imagination and inspires allegiance and devotion."

Recognize the Greatness in Others

18

I N Chapter 17 we described the power of having high expectations of your people and, more than once, strayed into talking about the importance of recognition in driving engagement, productivity, and charisma. However, we felt that there was not enough discussion in that chapter about the sort of recognition not specifically associated with the aim of raising people's expectations of themselves. Very simple forms of recognition have an extraordinarily charismatic impact on people – and, as a result, on their productivity.

What we're talking about in this chapter are not formal employee recognition schemes and programs – though they do, of course, have their place. We're talking about the potentially much more impactful recognition of a respected leader.

Quite apart from the fact that it is a clearly observable fact that those who are considered to be charismatic spend a lot of time in recognition and praise of others, there's a huge body of hard research that shows the direct impact of recognition on employee engagement and productivity.

One study by Towers Watson showed that supervisor recognition could raise engagement by as much as 60 percent. And, as discussed in Chapter 1, raising engagement dramatically raises productivity and bottom-line results.

According to a study undertaken by and Michael Treacy (author of *Double Digit Growth: How Some Companies Achieve It – No Matter What*) and Hewitt Associates:

> [M]anagers in double-digit companies will be most successful in improving engagement through recognizing their employee's achievements, and showing how those achievements lead to greater opportunities for the employee.

O.C. Tanner Company found the following:

Of the people who report the highest morale at work, 94.4% agree that their managers are effective at recognition. In contrast, 56% of employees who report low morale give their manager a failing grade on recognition.

It's clear – recognition contributes strongly to both employee engagement and bottom lines.

Brains, like hearts, go where they are appreciated.
— Robert McNamara, former US secretary of defense
and president, World Bank

Why Does Recognition Work?

Recognition is extremely powerful because it triggers two powerful physiological responses that are shared by every human being.

Physiology and Recognition: It's Chemical!

When you receive praise and recognition from another person, particularly someone who has your respect, your brain responds physiologically with a release of the brain's feel-good chemical dopamine. This is the chemical that gives the runner his or her high, those in love their intense feelings of well-being, and even provides the highly pleasurable feeling you get from eating chocolate or making love. Without dopamine it's pretty much impossible to feel pleasure.

In their article "In Praise of Praising Your Employees," *Gallup Management Journal* reported:

Recognition for good work releases Dopamine in the brain, which creates feelings of pride and pleasure. Better yet, that Dopamine hit cements the knowledge that more of that behavior will create more praise, resulting in another Dopamine drench, and so on.

This is why recognition is so effective. People will alter their behavior to achieve more recognition if it will result in the release of more dopamine. This is the same addictive response the brain has to love, chocolate, exercise, and even hard drugs.

Recognition works because our brain chemistry is wired to respond positively to it.

But there's another psychological factor that multiplies the effectiveness of recognition – the so-called "norm of reciprocity."

Psychology and Recognition: The "Norm of Reciprocity"

Why do salespeople on cosmetics counters give away expensive free samples? Why does the Hare Krishna follower give you a free book or a plastic flower? Why do cash-strapped charities often give away items like pens?

Simply because they expect you to respond in kind, returning favor for favor. The Hare Krishna follower gives you your free book and then solicits a donation; the cosmetics salesperson provides your free sample and then makes you a special offer of something else. The charity sends you the free pen with the appeal for a donation.

Why? Because it works! Most people naturally feel a sense of obligation when someone treats them kindly. People will often go along with requests from others who have done them some service, however small – even when that service was unsolicited, and even if the person rendering that service is someone they do not like.

This universal human response is called the "norm of reciprocity" and it is triggered just as naturally in people when the person who leads them gives them the "gift" of recognition.

When you show recognition to one of your people you trigger this normal human response, making it easier to get their cooperation in doing what you need to get done.

So recognition works in two important ways: conditioning those receiving it to repeat the behavior that won the recognition, and triggering an obligation to return the favor.

And the good news is: no one is immune to recognition! Some need it more than others, but we all genuinely crave it – regardless of our level of power or success. In fact, for those who are considered to be the best in their game, compliments, flattery, and recognition are frequently in short supply. After all, people know they are the best and assume that *they* know it well enough not to need such recognition. Wrong! Positive recognition works up, down, and sideways in the chain of command.

We all enjoy a stroke, and we are naturally drawn to those who pile recognition on us and repelled by those who either fail to provide it, or worse, intentionally withhold it from us.

There is no duty more indispensable than that of returning a kindness. All men distrust one forgetful of a benefit.
— Cicero, politician and philosopher

Recognition and Charisma

Understanding that everyone needs recognition and positive attention is another positive step on the road to developing real charisma. Making the decision to do whatever you can to provide that recognition is the logical next step.

Every interaction you have with someone is an opportunity to raise your charismatic appeal – by finding a genuine opportunity to provide recognition and raise that person's self-esteem.

Remember the Charismatic Equation we first defined earlier?

> The extent to which you are perceived as being charismatic is directly proportional to the extent to which people either feel or fare better after each and every interaction with you.

Become someone whom others associate with the shot of feel-good dopamine your positive recognition shoots into their brain and you become instantly much more charismatic to them.

Practical Recognition

Recognition can be as simple as treating people as equals and allowing them those everyday courtesies that can enhance their self-esteem.

Be Even Handed

Before getting into some practical ideas for daily recognition of your people, it is key to emphasize what should be an obvious point: to be effective, recognition must be seen to be even handed and fair. It must also be warranted.

You cannot afford to have favorites. You must ensure that all members of your team get equal opportunities for recognition when it's warranted. Withholding justified recognition from one person while lavishing it on another has an exponentially worse impact than providing no recognition at all.

Everyone who merits recognition should get it – and you should be continually on the lookout for ways in which every member of your team can be deemed to warrant it. Be careful, however, not to fall into the trap of providing recognition to anyone simply for recognition's sake – because it's their turn. If you heap shallow flattery on people then you devalue your recognition currency completely. Recognition must be earned.

Here's a buffet of effective recognition gestures that you should mix and match to ensure that everyone on your team gets appropriate recognition for results delivered – as often as possible.

Catch Them Doing Something Right

In Ken Blanchard's classic book *The One Minute Manager*, he advises that leaders not wait until they stumble across their people doing something well – but instead set out deliberately to catch them in the act.

Once you catch someone doing something particularly well, lavish praise and positive feedback on them. Ensure that, on a regular basis, you praise them in front of valued colleagues – those whom they would wish to impress. Public praise and recognition is the *crème de la crème* of recognition. There is nothing that has the same impact as genuine warranted praise in a forum of one's superiors and peers.

Listen

Really listen to other people. Genuinely focus on what they are saying, and provide frequent feedback in the form of eye contact, nods, and smiles to acknowledge key points. The mere act of deciding to focus and hear exactly what the other person is saying sets you up so that you will automatically establish positive eye contact – which is powerful recognition in itself (see Chapter 9).

One of the things remarked on more than anything else when people talk about meeting charismatic leaders is how they feel that they get 100 percent of their attention. Charismatics make those they speak with feel like they're the only people in the room. Giving someone your complete attention is a very powerful charismatic act.

Talking about Scott Cook, the charismatic founder of Intuit, *Inc.* magazine editor Michael Hopkins observed that "in conversation he still listens unlike any leader I have ever seen. Listening, he seems to forget himself."

When you are with someone, be with him or her. Don't allow your eyes to wander to other things going on around you; this signals indifference and can be unconsciously demeaning. Looking past someone or focusing on the "middle distance" signals total lack of interest and can even suggest arrogance. This is especially so if the one denying full attention is in a position of greater authority.

Arrogance is the complete opposite of charisma. Give your full attention and signal that attention with your eyes.

If someone does interrupt you, do not immediately steal your eyes away. Maintaining eye contact, excuse yourself, briefly deal with the interruption, and then resume your conversation with normal eye contact. A brief or even sustained touch to the lower arm of your conversational partner maintains a strong connection as you address such interruptions.

Know Their Strengths and Development Areas

Do you know all about the strengths, development needs, and priorities of each and every member of your team? If not, then review the section entitled "It's All about Them" in Chapter 13.

Know the true strengths of your people, and know what they regard as their strengths – those parts of their skills and personality of which they are proudest. Then, as often as possible, catch them applying both the strengths they recognize and those they don't. When you recognize them doing well using an unrecognized strength, or making progress in a development area, the praise and recognition will trigger the dopamine that makes them want to repeat that behavior.

Give Them Responsibility

Once you know what their particular strengths are, and their passions, go out of your way to find key responsibilities you can delegate to them that will help them to exercise the strengths they value, develop those they'd like to have, and exercise any work-related passions. When you find out what they feel really passionate about doing, give them the responsibility that allows them to do it.

Give Them Time

The time of a leader, especially that of a respected charismatic leader, is powerful recognition currency. As discussed in Chapter 13, schedule regular one-on-one sessions with each member of your team – to talk generally and to provide coaching and guidance. Not only will it enhance their expectations of themselves in the way discussed in that chapter, but it will also send a strong recognition message.

Keep Them Involved

There is no more powerful recognition than to be valued for your opinions and ideas. Seek frequent feedback and input, and get everyone involved in helping you make critical decisions from time to time. This is most effective if you do it on a one-on-one basis – as opposed to a committee-style decision process. When making a critical decision, call one person to the side and ask for input.

Promote Their Ideas

When you get useful feedback and ideas, give full credit to whomever provided them – again, in a public forum. Look for frequent input from all of your people, and, if a member of your team is trying to promote some particular idea that you feel has merit, be seen publicly to throw your weight behind him or her. This is powerful recognition.

Know Something about Their Non-Work Lives

What's important to them outside of work? What are their personal aspirations?

What's their family situation? What pastimes are they passionate about? Showing an interest in them that goes beyond the obvious work environment and topics is powerful recognition. Show an interest by asking about non work-related aspects of their lives.

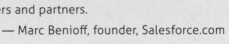

I believe a balanced life is essential, and I try to make sure that all of our employees know that and live that way. It's crucial that I help ensure that our employees are as successful as our customers and partners.

— Marc Benioff, founder, Salesforce.com

Ask for Favors

When a leader asks a subordinate for help with something, especially something that is clearly part of the subordinate's responsibilities anyway, the leader provides potent recognition of that person as an individual. Being asked for help flatters and makes another feel valued. When the person requesting that help is a leader, it is even more flattering.

Don't Keep Them Waiting

You are busy. All leaders are. Sometimes you cannot respond to your team's phone and e-mail messages as quickly as you'd like to. Keeping people waiting is the precise opposite of recognition – it undermines and demeans. If you're too busy to respond fully straight away, respond with a one-liner saying so.

Give Recognition, Get Charisma

The quotation below from Professor Jean-Pierre Brun says it all. The decision to give all of your people daily recognition is a decision to have a greater impact on their lives than you could possibly imagine.

Not only will your "small gestures" of recognition make your people feel more valued, drive engagement, and positively impact your bottom line, they'll also significantly advance your goal of becoming a charismatic leader.

> There are three great moments of recognition – at birth, at retirement and at death. Between those moments, recognition must be a daily affair, with small gestures. People aren't looking for remuneration as much as they are looking for simple acknowledgement.
>
> Recognition not only has a great impact on employee mental health, it also encourages the investment that employees make in their work. Recognition must be part of an ongoing, long-term process.
>
> — Jean-Pierre Brun, professor of management,
> Laval University, Quebec

So Where Now?

19

S o NOW YOU know everything that modern research can tell you about how to become a successful charismatic leader. You have information that will enable you not only to achieve extraordinary results from your people but also to create and maintain the sort of persona that characterizes so many of the world's great leaders, past and present.

What will you do now? If you take the advice in Chapter 2 (under "Raising Your Leadership Charisma: Getting the Most from This Book") you'll commit to the process and start working through the four steps systematically, chapter by chapter, from front to back, first creating a superior self-confident platform. You will then build magnetic physical charisma and engaging charismatic leader behaviors on that platform.

Work through the process systematically and we *guarantee* that you will see a dramatic increase in your charismatic impact on all those you encounter. Greatly improved business results will follow unavoidably as your people become more engaged with you and your vision than you ever thought possible. This is undoubtedly the most efficient and effective way of using this book.

But maybe you don't want to take this systematic approach. Perhaps you're impatient to put one or other of the ideas in the book to work right away. That's no problem. Every one of the 18 chapters is completely autonomous. Each provides practical ideas and suggestions on improving one particular aspect of leadership charisma. Pick the chapter that appeals to you most. Read it several times, and then commit to applying the lessons from that chapter over the following month. In your Haney-Sirbasku System (Chapter 6), or somewhere else you'll see it daily, write a note to remind you what chapter you are focusing on at any point in time – and then look for as many opportunities as possible to apply the ideas from that chapter every day of that month.

By the end of the first month you'll have made the practices in that first chapter a habit. They'll start to become a natural part of the way you do things (as you'll remember, according to Maxwell Maltz, it takes 21 days to make any practice a habit). That's the time to choose another chapter that particularly appeals to you and repeat the approach of focusing on applying that chapter's lessons throughout the following month.

Take this approach and in 18 months' time you'll have worked your way through the entire book without a huge amount of effort. You'll have established dozens of new habits that will have dramatically increased your leadership charisma, which will be evident in the greatly improved results you are achieving from your people.

Now that you know how you can be one of those striking, inspiring, and highly successful charismatic leaders admired by all … are you ready to take the first step?

You see, in life, lots of people know what to do, but few people actually do what they know.

Knowing is not enough!

You must take action.

— Anthony Robbins, entrepreneur and author

Appendix I

The DNA of Leadership Charisma: The Research

Charismatic leaders create and maintain a work environment where people are emotionally and intellectually committed to the organization's goals. They build an energetic and positive attitude in others and inspire them to do their very best. In doing so they create a common sense of purpose in which people are more inclined to invest extra energy and even some of their own time in their work.

HAVING DEFINED THE very practical commercial form of charisma discussed in Chapter 1, we had to figure out precisely what it was that those who were considered charismatic leaders did to be perceived in this way. We had to identify precisely what behaviors generated leadership charisma, so that others could learn to assimilate those behaviors and increase it in themselves.

Not only that, but we had to work out a means to measure an individual leader's level of leadership charisma – his or her "leadership charisma quotient" – so that leaders wishing to raise the charismatic impact of their approach would have a metric that would allow them to measure how they were progressing toward that goal.

To achieve all this we had to launch what we believe is the largest study ever undertaken on the topic of charisma in leadership.

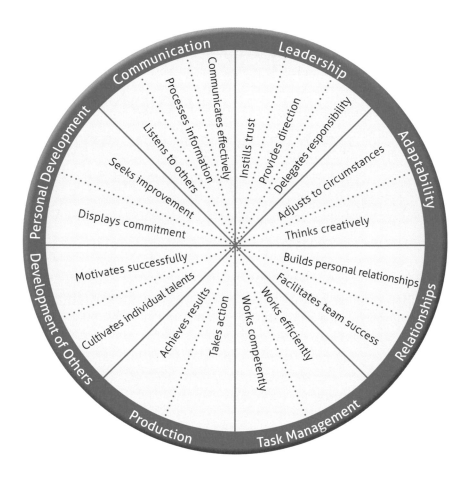

Figure 4: Checkpoint Leadership Model: top two levels.

Leadership Charisma Research

Before conducting serious research on what behaviors drive leadership charisma, we had to identify a model that covered all of the key behaviors that drive excellent leader performance in general.

Profiles International (www.profilesinternational.com) began to develop the Checkpoint Leadership Model in 1996. Their objective was to formulate a set of universal leadership behaviors that could be used to describe what top-performing managers and leaders do better than their average peers – those behaviors that make their performance superior. A critical goal in the development of Checkpoint was to describe what behaviors are required for top performance in any management or leadership position – regardless of country, language, or industry.

Since 1996 this 70-behavior leadership model has undergone continual research and development. Over that period more than 12 million leaders in 120 countries have had their leadership capabilities assessed using this competency model. Profiles International currently assesses several hundred thousand leaders against this model annually. Those assessments are carried out in more than 120 countries and in 40 languages. This is a leadership competency assessment and development model with a truly global pedigree.

The top two levels of the Checkpoint Leadership Model are shown in Figure 4 above. You can see that the top level consists of eight skill groups, which themselves are broken down into 18 sub-skill groups. Those 18 sub-skill groups break down in turn to the 70 very specific leadership competencies shown below.

Communication

Listens to others

1. Solicits ideas, suggestions, and opinions from others.
2. Creates a comfortable climate for airing concerns.
3. Listens to all points of view with an open mind.
4. Listens carefully without interrupting.
5. Summarizes input, then checks for understanding.

Processes information

6. Identifies the core element of an issue.
7. Considers the pros and cons, as well as short-term and long-

term consequences, of decisions.

8. Arrives at logical, clear conclusions.

Communicates effectively

9. Expresses thoughts clearly in writing.

10. Is an effective, articulate speaker.

11. Covers an issue thoroughly without overdoing it.

12. Communicates in a straightforward manner, even when dealing with sensitive topics.

13. Makes current job-related information readily available to others.

Leadership

Instills trust

14. Keeps promises.

15. Can be trusted with confidential information.

16. Is honest in dealings with others.

17. Demonstrates high ethical standards.

Provides direction

18. Makes expectations clear.

19. Establishes a manageable workload.

20. Accomplishes long-term objectives by planning and taking the necessary steps.

21. Keeps focus on the big picture while implementing details.

Delegates responsibility

22. Knows when to delegate and when to assume responsibility.

23. Delegates the right jobs to the right people.

24. Gives others authority to fulfill responsibilities independently.

25. Empowers others to find creative solutions to problems.

Adaptability

Adjusts to circumstances

26. Is flexible in dealing with people with diverse work styles.
27. Is comfortable in a variety of environments.
28. Reacts constructively to setbacks.
29. Anticipates and plans for changing situations.

Thinks creatively

30. Approaches the job with imagination and originality.
31. Inspires innovation in the organization.
32. Is willing to take bold, calculated risks.
33. Views obstacles as opportunities for creative change.

Relationships

Builds personal relationships

34. Shows consideration for the feelings of others.
35. Does not think, speak or act according to prejudiced or stereo-typical ideas.
36. Delivers criticism tactfully and constructively.
37. Maintains composure in high-pressure situations.

Facilitates team success

38. Resolves conflicts fairly.
39. Creates an atmosphere of cooperation instead of competition within a team.
40. Builds consensus on decisions.
41. Leads the team in formulating goals that complement the organization's mission.
42. Brings capable people into the group.
43. Uses the diverse talents and experiences of the group to maximum advantage.

Task management

Works efficiently

44. Applies current technology in practical ways to maximize efficiency.
45. Makes wise use of outside resources.
46. Avoids procrastination.
47. Sets priorities and tackles assignments accordingly.

Works competently

48. Demonstrates mastery of the fundamentals necessary to the job.
49. Is skilled at learning and applying new information quickly.
50. Integrates new theories, trends, and methods into appropriate business operations.

Production

Takes action

51. Knows when to stop planning and start implementing.
52. Takes the initiative to make things happen.
53. Is assertive in managing problems.
54. Makes timely, clear-cut, firm decisions.

Achieves results

55. Overcomes obstacles to complete projects successfully.
56. Effects outcomes that set high standards for others.
57. Achieves results that have a positive impact on the organization as a whole.

Development of others

Cultivates individual talents

58. Is a patient, helpful, effective coach.

59. Gives others access to training for skill development and professional growth.
60. Provides objective appraisals of the strengths and needs of others.
61. Maintains a timely schedule for reviews and follow-ups.

Motivates successfully

62. Gives recognition to producers of high-quality work.
63. Shows appreciation when others give extra effort.
64. Shares a contagious enthusiasm that promotes a positive attitude in others.

Personal development

Displays commitment

65. Maintains a consistently high energy level.
66. Persists and perseveres.
67. Keeps a positive outlook.

Seeks improvement

68. Admits mistakes and learns from them.
69. Accepts constructive criticism.
70. Identifies and pursues resources needed to improve performance.

This model clearly covers all of the critical factors that drive excellence in leadership performance, and so it was an ideal template for this study. However, an even more important strength of this model is that all 70 behaviors had been carefully designed and refined so that they are crystal clear in their meaning – and all could be developed by anyone prepared to invest the time and effort in doing so.

Checkpoint uses a multi-rater/360-degree feedback approach to assess the perception of a leader's performance. Using the 70 specific leadership behaviors, leaders are rated by four audiences in their organizations, offering a complete picture of the perception of the leaders' skills. Those four raters are:

1. **Self**

   The leader assesses his or her own perception of his or her performance against the 70 Checkpoint behaviors.

2. **Boss**

   The direct superior of the leader being assessed rates the leader's performance on the 70 behaviors.

3. **Direct reports**

   Those who report directly to the leader provide their perspective on the leader's performance against the 70 Checkpoint behaviors.

4. **Peers**

   Finally, the leader is assessed by peer-level colleagues in his or her organization – fellow leaders on the same level.

Respondents from these four categories are asked to rate how often a leader displays the 70 behaviors, using a scale that runs from one to five as follows:

1. Never (displays the behavior).
2. Seldom (displays the behavior).
3. Sometimes (displays the behavior).
4. Often (displays the behavior).
5. Always (displays the behavior).

The result of a Checkpoint analysis of a leader is an enormous amount of information on what behaviors the assessed leader displays on a daily basis from the perspective of those who know best – those who interact most closely with him or her in the workplace.

This information is generally fed back to leaders being assessed in the form of a full-color report that gives them a comprehensive overview of how their perceptions of their own leadership compare with those of their boss, direct reports, and peers. A comprehensive analysis of particular strengths is provided, as is a prioritized listing of areas for development – those behaviors that leaders should work on in order to reach maximum effectiveness in their current positions. Finally, the report provides a customized four-page development plan to guide leaders on what to do to "raise their game."

Uniquely, the Checkpoint system also provides an "Organizational Management Analysis," combining the results of multiple leaders within an organization (at department, country, or whole-organization level) to provide a comprehensive overview of the strengths and development needs of a group of leaders as a whole.

As an online system with more than 20 years' history of ongoing use and development, this was the perfect platform for our research.

Making the Charisma Connection

As discussed above, Profiles put several hundred thousand leaders through the Checkpoint analysis on an annual basis, and, for a nine-month period in 2010, an additional item was added to the Checkpoint system. It was for completion by respondents after they had finished rating a leader on the 70 leadership behaviors.

Using our definition of leadership charisma, Profiles asked each respondent over that period to rate leaders on their charisma using a scale that ran from one to five. On that scale five was "high leadership charisma," three was "moderate leadership charisma," and one was "low leadership charisma." The study included participants from 120 countries worldwide. Having done this, we knew the extent to which these leaders were perceived as being charismatic.

Then, having both a rating from more than 400,000 people on the perceived charisma of their 40,000 leaders and a comprehensive picture of the behaviors each of those leaders was observed to demonstrate from day to day, we set out to correlate high-charisma scores with the behaviors displayed by those receiving them. In this way, we could determine precisely what behaviors these leaders demonstrated on a daily basis to create the perception of high leadership charisma.

Leadership Charisma Behaviors

We analyzed this data to determine which of the 70 Checkpoint behaviors had the most significant correlations with leader charisma. These results were exactly what we had hoped for. They provided a clear connection between specific learnable leadership behaviors and the perception of leadership charisma. The complete model for driving the step-by-step development of robust leadership charisma is described in detail in Chapter 2.

The research showed that some behaviors were more important than others in creating a charismatic impact on employees – in some cases dramatically so. Those six main behavior groups are listed in Table 1 below in the order of the magnitude of the impact they had on people's perception of leadership charisma. In each case the sub-skill groups that concerned charisma have been listed under the main group heading.

Leadership Charisma Behaviors

1. Communication
   - Listens to others.
   - Communicates effectively.

2. Development of others
   - Cultivates individual talents.
   - Motivates successfully.

3. Productivity
   - Takes action.

4. Relationships
   - Builds personal relationships.
   - Facilitates team success.

5. Adaptability
- Thinks creatively.

6. Personal development
- Displays commitment.
- Seeks improvement.

Table 1: Charismatic behaviors: The direct-report perspective.

These are the behaviors that will evoke a charismatic response to your leadership, and the ones that must define the way those who work for you would describe you if asked to do so.

This is what it takes to be charismatic in the eyes of your team members, and this is how you need to appear to them.

Appendix II
Sample Goal Word Picture

It is Christmas Day, 20XX.

How fantastically well 20XX turned out! I am so happy to be celebrating one of the most successful years of my life – ever!

Early in 20XX I broke my habit of worrying too much and instead made the firm decision to focus all of my efforts entirely on my goals. I have never been happier or more content. I am so much more self-assured and confident in myself and my future.

As a result of my soaring self-confidence I have developed a much more inspirational relationship with my team. I am becoming more charismatic and more inspirational. My people now view me as an inspiring and charismatic leader who makes an enormous difference in all that he does.

Sales doubled during 20XX thanks to the creative ways I came up with of generating even more prospects, despite the difficult economic conditions.

I am admired and respected by all for my extraordinary success in recreating my business and taking it to new heights.

I am stunned at how successful my expertise goal has been. Just by reading my one book weekly I already notice that I know more about our business than anyone I meet. Not just that, but harnessing that reading to write articles and create a blog has built me a serious reputation as an expert in this field – on an increasingly wide international basis.

I am more financially secure than I have ever been – and I am almost totally debt free. I have almost halved my mortgage and I'm on a path that will see it totally cleared in 20XX.

I have no financial worries either for now or for the future.

I have a very happy home life and a relationship with <partner's name> that is stronger and more passionate than ever. I also have a great relationship with <children's names>. I am a great father.

As a result of all of this I feel happier, more content, and more secure than I have ever felt in my life. I especially like the way my success in 20XX has left me feeling so light, positive, and energetic in all I do, all of the time.

I have no worries.

Life is good and getting better. Every day is an opportunity to improve my lot even further. The world is truly my oyster and I see nothing but great possibilities for the future.

I feel truly blessed.

Selected Bibliography

Books

Assaraf, John and Smith, Murray, *The Answer: Grow any Business, Achieve Financial Freedom, and Live an Extraordinary Life* (New York: Atria, 2008).

Baldwin, Robert and Paris, Ruth, *The Book of Similes* (London and Boston: Routledge and Kegan Paul, 1982).

Blanchard, Kenneth H. and Johnson, Spencer, *The One Minute Manager* (New York: Morrow, 1982).

Buckingham, Marcus, *The One Thing You Need to Know: About Managing, Great Leading, and Sustained Individual Success* (New York: Free Press, 2005).

Carnegie, Dale, *How to Win Friends and Influence People* (New York: Simon and Schuster, 1937).

Clarke, Arthur C., *Profiles of the Future: An Inquiry into the Limits of the Possible* (New York: Harper and Row, 1962).

Cohen, Steve, *Win the Crowd: Unlock the Secrets of Influence, Charisma, and Showmanship* (New York: HarperCollins, 2005).

Conger, Jay Alden, *The Charismatic Leader: Behind the Mystique of Exceptional Leadership* (San Francisco: Jossey-Bass Publishers, 1989).

Covey, Stephen R., *The 8th Habit: From Effectiveness to Greatness* (New York: Free Press, 2004).

Emison, Patricia A., *Growing with the Grain: Dynamic Families Shaping History from Ancient Times* (Lee, NH: Lady Illyria Press, 2005), p. 144.

Gebauer, Julie, Lowman, Don, and Gordon, Joanne, *Closing the Engagement Gap: How Great Companies Unlock Employee Potential for Superior Results* (New York: Portfolio, 2008).

Grant, Robert M. and Neupert, Kent E., *Cases in Contemporary Strategy Analysis* (Malden, MA: Blackwell, 1999).

Grothe, Mardy, *I Never Metaphor I Didn't Like: A Comprehensive Compilation of History's Greatest Analogies, Metaphors, and Similes* (New York: Collins, 2008).

Lipton, Mark, *Guiding Growth: How Vision Keeps Companies on Course* (Boston: Harvard Business School Press, 2003).

Love, Roger, *Love Your Voice: Use Your Speaking Voice to Create Success, Self-Confidence, and Star-Like Charisma!* (London: Hay House, 2008).

Lutz, William, *The New Doublespeak: Why No One Knows What Anyone's Saying Anymore* (New York: HarperCollins, 1996).

Powell, Colin and Persico, Joseph E., *My American Journey* (New York: Random House, 1995).

Rosenthal, Robert and Jacobson, Lenore, *Pygmalion in the Classroom: Teacher Expectation and Pupils' Intellectual Development* (New York: Holt, Rinehart and Winston, 1968).

Scott, Susan, *Fierce Leadership: A Bold Alternative to the Worst "Best" Practices of Business Today* (New York: Broadway Business, 2009).

Seligman, Martin E.P., *Learned Optimism* (New York: Knopf, 1990).

Silva, José and Miele, Philip, *The Silva Mind Control Method* (New York: Simon and Schuster, 1977).

Tesla, Nikola and Johnston, Ben, *My Inventions: The Autobiography of Nikola Tesla* (Williston, VT: Hart Brothers, 1982).

Treacy, Michael, *Double Digit Growth: How Some Companies Achieve It – No Matter What* (New York: Portfolio, 2003).

Turner, Ted with Burke, Bill, *Call Me Ted* (New York: Grand Central Publications, 2008).

Articles and Studies

Berglas, Steven, "What You Can Learn from Steve Jobs," *Inc.* (October 1999), http://tinyurl.com/32hut76.

Bezos, Jeff, "Inventing E-Commerce," *Academy of Achievement* (May 4, 2001), http://tinyurl.com/2crln63.

Bono, Joyce E. and Ilies, Remus, "Charisma, Positive Emotions and Mood Contagion," *Leadership Quarterly* **17** (4) (2006), pp. 317–34.

Butler, Timothy and Waldroop, James, "Job Sculpting," *Harvard Business Review* **77** (5) (September–October 1999), pp. 144–52.

Chandler, Michele, "Microsoft's Ballmer Says Nurturing Innovation and Top Talent Are Priorities," *Stanford GBS News* (September 2008), http://tinyurl.com/2uafudq.

Chartrand, Tanya and Bargh, John, "The Unbearable Automaticity of Being," *The American Psychologist* **54** (7) (1999), p. 462.

Coffman, Curt, "The High Cost of Disengaged Employees," *Gallup Management Journal* (April 15, 2002), http://tinyurl.com/2ecdr8z.

Dell, Michael S., "From Dorm Room to Board Room," *Academy of Achievement* (July 3, 2008), http://tinyurl.com/35kmmz4.

DePauw University, "New York Times Writes of Prof. Matt Hertenstein's Research on Communicating Via Touch," *DePauw University* (accessed September 27, 2010), http://tinyurl.com/38falpc.

Dimberg, Ulf, Thunberg, Monika, and Elmehed, Kurt, "Unconscious Facial Reactions to Emotional Facial Expressions," *Psychological Science: A Journal of the American Psychological Society* **11** (1) (2000), pp. 86–9.

Donahoe, John, "Code of Business Conduct and Ethics," *eBay* (accessed September 27, 2010), http://tinyurl.com/2wc49hz.

Donlon, J.P., "Are Your Employees Engaged?," *ChiefExecutive.net* (accessed September 27, 2010), http://tinyurl.com/zgy8k.

Eden, Dov, "Leadership and Expectations: Pygmalion Effects and Other Self-Fulfilling Prophecies in Organizations," *Leadership Quarterly* **3** (4) (winter 1992) pp. 271–305.

Friedman, H.S., Prince, L.M., Riggio, R.E., and DiMatteo, M.R., "Understanding and Assessing Nonverbal Expressiveness: The Affective Communication Test," *Journal of Personality and Social Psychology* **39** (September 2006), pp. 333–51.

Gallo, Carmine, "How Cisco's CEO Works the Crowd," *BusinessWeek* (October 11, 2006), http://tinyurl.com/dj5jgs.

Gallo, Carmine, "Storytelling Tips from Salesforce's Marc Benioff," *BusinessWeek* (November 3, 2009), http://tinyurl.com/y923wqb.

Gallo, Carmine, "The Napkin Test," *BusinessWeek* (December 7, 2007), http://tinyurl.com/33hpxht.

Gallo, Carmine, "Why Leadership Means Listening," *BusinessWeek* (January 31, 2007), http://tinyurl.com/rcbmea.

Gibbons, John M., "I Can't Get No ... Job Satisfaction, That Is," *The Conference Board* (January 2010), http://tinyurl.com/36zxrqq.

Google Inc., "Corporate Information," *Google* (2010), http://www.google.com/corporate.

Government of Nova Scotia, "Building a Business Case for Employee Recognition," *Government of Nova Scotia* (2006), http://tinyurl.com/28voveg.

Grugal, Robin, "Decide upon Your True Dreams and Goals: Corporate Culture Is the Key," *Investor's Business Daily* (April 15, 2003).

Hall, E.T., "A System for the Notation of Proxemic Behavior," *American Anthropologist* **65** (5) (1963), pp. 1,003–26.

Hopkins, Michael S., "Scott Cook, Intuit: Because He Learns, and Teaches," *Inc.* (April 2004), http://tinyurl.com/32u7pxr.

Horn, Brian, "Dressed for Success: How George Zimmer Created and Maintains a Culture that Drives Growth at Men's Wearhouse," *Smart Business Houston* (June 2009), http://tinyurl.com/2wbtvyn.

Kanter, Rosabeth Moss, "How Leaders Gain (and Lose) Confidence," *Leader to Leader Journal* **35** (winter 2005), pp. 21–7.

Kanungo, R.N. and Conger, Jay A., "Dimensions of Executive Charisma," *Vikalpa* **14** (4) (October–December 1989).

Kelly, Spencer D., Özyürek, Aslı, and Maris, Eric, "Two Sides of the Same Coin: Speech and Gesture Mutually Interact to Enhance Comprehension," *Psychological Science* **21** (2) (2010), pp. 260–67.

Khan, Adalat, "Employee Engagement a Winning Formula for Success," *American Chronicle* (September 4, 2007), http://tinyurl.com/28dzfbr.

Kroft, Steve, "Richard the Lionhearted," *60 Minutes*, CBS (1992), http://tinyurl.com/2ek42aa.

Kuhn, Cliff, "Mental Health," *natural-humor-medicine.com* (accessed September 27, 2010), http://tinyurl.com/2wtbtj7.

Lafley, A.G., "What Only the CEO Can Do," *Harvard Business Review* **87** (5) (May 2009).

Lipton, Mark, "Walking the Talk (Really!): Why Visions Fail," *Ivey Business Journal* (January/February 2004), http://tinyurl.com/mbntv5.

Livingston, J. Sterling, "Pygmalion in Management," *Harvard Business Review* **81** (1) (Jan 2003), pp. 97–106.

Matthews, Gail, "Goals Research Summary," *Dominican University of California* (accessed September 27, 2010), http://tinyurl.com/23t4qo6.

Naidoo, L.J. and Lord, R.G., "Speech Imagery and Perceptions of Charisma: The Mediating Role of Positive Affect," *Leadership Quarterly* **19** (3) (2008), p. 283 ff.

Ransdell, Eric, "They Sell Suits With Soul," *Fast Company* **18** (September 1998).

Robinson, Jennifer, "In Praise of Praising Your Employees," *Gallup Management Journal* (November 9, 2006), http://tinyurl.com/38soweh.

Schnake, M.E., Dumler, M.P., Cochran, D.S., and Barnett, T.R., "Effects of Differences in Superior and Subordinate Perceptions of Superiors' Communication Practices," *Journal of Business Communication* **27** (1) (winter 1990), pp. 37–50.

Sonshi.com, "Interview with Marc Benioff," *Sonshi.com* (accessed September 27, 2010), http://tinyurl.com/34v9rrs.

Strohmeier, Brian R., "The Leadership Principles Used by Jack Welch as he Re-energized, Revolutionized, and Reshaped General Electric," *Journal of Leadership and Organizational Studies* **5** (2) (1998), pp. 16–26.

Townsend, Heather, "Why Your Handshake Could Be Damaging Your Reputation," *The Efficiency Coach* (March 16, 2010), http://tinyurl.com/yehd4u4.

Treacy, Michael and Hewitt Associates, "Research Brief: Employee Engagement Higher at Double-Digit Growth Companies," *Hewitt Associates* (2004), http://tinyurl.com/3xdz22o.

Unknown, "On the Record: David Neeleman," *San Francisco Chronicle* (September 12, 2004).

Welch, Jack, "Are Leaders Born or Made?," *The Welch Way* (December 19, 2005), http://tinyurl.com/ckyh5v.